Why Grow Up?

Why Grow Up?

SUBVERSIVE THOUGHTS FOR
AN INFANTILE AGE

Susan Neiman

FARRAR, STRAUS AND GIROUX

NEW YORK

Farrar, Straus and Giroux
18 West 18th Street, New York 10011

Library of Congress Cataloging-in-Publication Data
Neiman, Susan.
    Why grow up? : subversive thoughts for an infantile age / Susan
Neiman. — First American edition.
        pages   cm
    Includes bibliographical references and index.
    ISBN 978-0-374-28996-6 (hardcover) — ISBN 978-0-374-71320-1
(e-book)
    1. Maturation (Psychology)   I. Title.

BF710 .N44 2015
155.2'5—dc23

                                                    2014039383

www.fsgbooks.com
www.twitter.com/fsgbooks • www.facebook.com/fsgbooks

1   3   5   7   9   10   8   6   4   2

For Leila

Contents

Introduction

You need not be Peter Pan to feel uneasy about the prospect of becoming adult. Indeed, it's easy to argue that Peter Pan, most drastically imitated by Michael Jackson, is an emblem of our times. Being grown-up is widely considered to be a matter of renouncing your hopes and dreams, accepting the limits of the reality you are given, and resigning yourself to a life that will be less adventurous, worthwhile and significant than you supposed when you began it. Simone de Beauvoir ended the third volume of her autobiography with the reflection that there wasn't much of the world she hadn't seen: 'the opera of Peking, the arena of the Huelva, the dunes of El Oued, the dawns in Provence, Castro talking to five hundred thousand Cubans, the white nights of Leningrad, an orange moon over the Piraeus'. Not only did she travel the world at a time when, unlike ours, such travel could hardly be taken for granted; the loves and friendships, the meaningful work and the acclaim she received for it were nearly as numerous and varied as the places she saw. It's hard to imagine a life more full or less wasted. Yet she concludes the enviable list of her travels with a look back at the girl she once was, 'gazing at the gold mine at my feet: a whole life to live', and concludes that she was cheated. Some writers argue that few people these days *want* to grow up. But if adulthood is a matter of feeling, in one's more honest moments, that one was cheated, who can blame them?

Can philosophy help us to find a model of maturity that is not a matter of resignation? (For the record, my *Oxford Thesaurus* lists 'philosophical' as a synonym for 'resigned'.) I believe that it can, and the best place to begin is Immanuel Kant's description of the process of reason's coming of age towards the end of the *Critique of Pure Reason*. Readers may be forgiven for ignoring it. The *Critique of Pure Reason* (1781) is at once the most important and the worst-written book in the history of modern philosophy. Kant himself wrote that it was too long and too dry, before poignantly adding that it is 'not given to everyone to write so subtly and gracefully as David Hume, or so profoundly and elegantly as Moses Mendelssohn'. True enough. Bertrand Russell was not the only reader to admit to falling asleep before he reached the end. Those who persevere, however, will find that his model of coming of age can be very compelling.

The infancy of reason is dogmatic. Small children incline to take what they are given as absolute truth. What perspective would allow them to question it? Those who suffer abuse at the hands of parental or priestly authority need years to realize that abuse is not simply part of the furniture of the universe – if they ever realize it at all. In happier cases, each step the child takes seems to confirm both her own powers and the transparency of a world that initially seemed mysterious. She learns that spoons (and rattles and pudding) regularly fall down and not up when you drop them, that balls (and trucks and kittens) are objects that persist even when they roll behind the curtain. As her own capacities grow, the world becomes increasingly comprehensible. Why shouldn't she assume that both are unlimited? Each day she understands a little more, each day another secret of her world is unravelled. For the small child, the dogmatic metaphysics of the seventeenth-century philosopher and consummate optimist Leibniz will seem obvious: had we but world enough and time, we would be able to know everything – and to understand that this world is the best of all possible ones. What else would make sense?

The next step of reason is scepticism, and though the word 'adolescence' was not invented in Kant's day, he describes all its symptoms: the peculiar mixture of disappointment and exhilaration that accompanies the teenager's discovery that the world is not the way it should be. Even at their very best – and we seldom are – parents and teachers have failings. (And those of us who have become parents and teachers ourselves have also been adolescents, just as surely as the rest of you.) They know less than we thought they did, they can offer fewer solutions than we hoped.

Even when they do not lie, they did not tell us all they could have; they want to shield us in the wrong ways and fail to protect us in the right ones. They embarrass us with habits and beliefs they inevitably acquired in an earlier era; they criticize what they don't understand and hang on to times that have changed. Why shouldn't we conclude that whatever truths and rules we learned from them were misguided; indeed, that the very ideas of truth and rule deserve to be laid to rest? Why shouldn't we move from boundless trust in the world to boundless mistrust?

Kant says this step is more mature than the wide-eyed credulity of reason's childhood, and therefore necessary and valuable. (To be sure, he never had to raise an adolescent.) But the wild swing from endless trust to permanent distrust is not yet maturity. Unsurprisingly, maturity is Kant's metaphor for his own philosophy, which should give you the wisdom to find a path between mindlessly accepting everything you're told and mindlessly rejecting it. Growing up is a matter of acknowledging the uncertainties that weave through our lives; often worse, of living without certainty while recognizing that we will inevitably continue to seek it. Such a standpoint is easier to describe than to consistently maintain, but then again, whoever said growing up would be easy?

The problem with all this, at first glance, is not that it's hard but that it's boring. Worse than boring, it sounds resigned. Is there more to this standpoint than you could get from your harmless but well-meaning uncle, growing a belly, who tells you that life will be neither as wondrous as you thought in your childhood nor as tormented as you thought in your adolescence, and it's time to buck up and make the best of it? Banal as it is, this statement is true, but it hardly seems worth striving for. Why not just skip Kant and listen to the Rolling Stones? If you try sometimes, you just might find you get what you need. And speaking of harmless uncles: Kant's life hardly seems a model of an adulthood to which you'd aspire. He never travelled further than forty miles from the place he was born, he never married; even the one rumour we have of a love affair remains unconfirmed. His adult life consisted of a routine of lectures, academic chores and writing so demanding and regular that his neighbours were said to set their watches by the daily walk he took to maintain his weak constitution. The poet Heinrich Heine went so far as to say that Kant's life-history was easy to describe, for he had neither a life nor a history.

That same poet, however, also described Kant as a rebel who stormed the heavens and made the French revolutionary Robespierre seem humdrum. Nor was Heine alone. Most of Kant's younger contemporaries felt much the same. We begin to see why when we turn to Kant's most famous discussion of maturity, which occurs at the beginning of the Enlightenment's best-known essay. 'What is Enlightenment?' (1784)

defines it as reason's emancipation from its self-incurred immaturity. We choose immaturity because we are lazy and scared: how much more comfortable it is to let someone else make your decisions! 'If I have a book that takes care of my understanding, a preacher who takes care of my conscience, a doctor who prescribes my diet, I need not make any effort myself. I need not think, so long as I can pay; others will handle the business for me.' (Even Kant could write straightforward sentences when he was writing for the *Berlinische Monatsschrift*, the eighteenth century's version of *The New York Review of Books*.) With a familiarity surprising in a man who had no children, Kant describes the way they learn to walk. In order to do so they must stumble and fall, but preventing bruises by keeping them in a baby carriage is a recipe for keeping them infantile. Kant's target, of course, is not over-protective mothers, but authoritarian states, for whom grown-up citizens are far more trouble than they're worth. The state's desire for control and our own desire for comfort combine to create societies with fewer conflicts, but they are not societies of grown-ups.

Growing up is more a matter of courage than knowledge: all the information in the world is no substitute for the guts to use your own judgement. And judgement can be learned – principally through the experience of watching others use it well – but it cannot be taught. Judgement is important because none of the answers to the questions that really move us can be found by following a rule. Courage is not only required to learn how to trust your own judgement rather than relying on your state's, your neighbour's or your favourite movie star's. (Of course, your state, your neighbour or your favourite movie star may often be right, and good judgement requires you to recognize *that*.) Even more important, courage is required to live with the rift that will run through our lives, however good they may be: ideals of reason tell us how the world should be; experience tells us that it rarely is. Growing up requires confronting the gap between the two – without giving up on either one.

Most of us are tempted to give up on one or the other. People who stick to the dogmas of childhood can spend whole lifetimes denying that the world does not conform to beliefs they hold dear. While examples of these abound – certain preachers and politicians come to mind – in our day it's more common to meet people who are stuck in the mire of adolescence. The world turns out not to reflect the ideas and ideals they had for it? All the worse for ideals. Maintaining ideals in a world that seems to have no use for them becomes a source of disappointment, even shame. Far better to jettison them entirely than to suffer the memory of hope defeated; far braver to face the depth of the rot of reality than to cling to what turned out to be illusion.

Such a standpoint is less brave than you think, for it

7

demands absolutely nothing but an air of urbanity. Far more courage is needed to acknowledge that both ideals and experience make equal claims on us. Growing up is a matter of respecting those claims and meeting them as best you can, knowing you will never succeed entirely but refusing to succumb to dogma or despair. If you live long enough, each will probably tempt you. Doing what you can to move your part of the world closer to the way that it should be, while never losing sight of the way that it is, is what being a grown-up comes to. If you happen to have a portly uncle who taught you that, you are very lucky.

But enough, for the moment, of reason. There are precious few points of consensus in modern Western philosophy, and one of them is that both reason and experience play a role in most of what you learn. Here again, Kant was decisive. Rationalists like Descartes pointed out the ways in which our senses deceive us, and argued that reason alone could be relied on to tell the truth about the world. Hadn't physics just discovered that things like colours were merely properties and not part of the essence of matter? Hadn't mathematics begun to sound the depths of the universe? Empiricists like Locke, by contrast, called the mind a *tabula rasa*, a slate that stays blank until experience writes upon it. Locke's heir, David Hume, went so far as to call reason impotent. Most philosophers today hold Kant to have ended two centuries of debate by showing that both reason *and* experience are needed for knowledge. As he put it, concepts without experience are empty, experience without concepts, blind. Such debates can always be, and have been revived, but it's interesting to note that most contemporary neuroscience supports the spirit, if not the letter, of Kant's view. Experiments show that certain experiences actually change the shape of your brain, just as internal mental frameworks are crucial in shaping your experience. The ways in which both reason and experience affect our coming of age will be a theme that runs through this book.

What kinds of experiences are crucial for growing up? To be attuned to the way the world is, you have to have seen something of it. Though philosophers like Blaise Pascal and Lao Tzu thought you could learn all you need to know inside your own room, many have thought travel to be crucial. For example, Kant's lectures on anthropology tell us that travel is a very good means of learning about human beings, provided one has first got to know one's own country-folk.

But wait, you may ask. *Didn't you just tell us that he never travelled more than forty miles from Königsberg?*

Don't forget that travel was a different experience in those days. Bumping in a coach over stony excuses for roads. Ears alert for the footfall of bandits and highwaymen. Uncertain inns over weeks and weeks and weeks. And that was just to get from Weimar to Sicily, which was the great journey in the life of Kant's more adventurous – and more privileged – younger compatriot Johann Wolfgang Goethe. But even Goethe could only dream of going any further.

Still, bad roads are a bad excuse, if Kant's own lectures on anthropology make such an argument for the benefits of travel!

There is, of course, a difference between theory and practice. That Kant himself felt abashed about his inability to live out his own suggestion is clear from a footnote to the passage on travel – the only unintentionally *ad hominem* and funny argument I ever found in his works.

A large city, the center of a realm, where the offices of the government are located, that has a university (to cultivate the sciences) and on top of it all has a harbor for sea-trade, which enables traffic not only to the interior of the country but also to neighboring countries with different languages and customs – such a city, as for example Königsberg on the river Pregel, can serve as an appropriate place for extending one's knowledge of humankind as well as the world, where knowledge can be acquired without traveling. (*Anthropology from a Pragmatic Point of View*, p. 4)

It sounds like special pleading, but could it be true? There may be some people, in some places, whose minds are so broad and open they need not go far to fill them. Kant might have been such a person, and any of those who are reading these words on one screen or another might be too. Doesn't the internet offer more space and time than humankind ever dreamed? If you spend your time in cyberspace watching something besides porn and Korean rap videos, you can gain a great deal. You can read news from hundreds of sources across the world, and learn how differently the same event can be reported. Alas, several recent studies have shown that the internet makes most of us narrower. We read the blogs and the websites that our friends read, limiting our perspective yet further, but the possibilities for expansion are evident. The Arab Spring, whatever its consequences, allowed us to glimpse them, and there's nothing to be said against an occasional Korean rap video either. Who knew?

But those who have lived, and especially worked, for long enough in another language and in another country than the one they were born into know how much others miss. Even mastery of a language won't give you the allusions – to the children's lullabies, for instance, that your new compatriots fell asleep to, and will never entirely get out of their heads. You'll miss jokes and nuances and much of the irony. (English-speaking Dylan fans will groan at the fact that a German women's magazine recently named 'Boots of Spanish Leather' as the optimal song for long-distance relationships.) Thus travel in places other than cyberspace has often been seen as a crucial step along the path to coming of age. The practice of sending poor men's sons off to apprenticeships is now much rarer in Europe than it used to be, but it's alive and well in places like Tunisia and the Philippines. Wealthier children – who are as likely, these days, to come from Moscow or Beijing as from London or New York – are still sent on one or another version of what the nineteenth century knew as the Grand Tour. In Europe, where the practice is meant to strengthen the political union, it's called the Erasmus programme; in America it is known as the junior year abroad.

According to some recent studies, the Erasmus programme may not contribute as much to European integration as it's meant to; many students report coming back with the feeling that their ties to their home countries have been strengthened. But as a step to coming of age it works significantly better than the study abroad programmes of most American colleges, if only because Europeans consider it ill-bred to speak just one language. Former Harvard president Larry Summers recently told the *New York Times* that learning a second language was a waste of time that could better be spent maximizing something quantifiable. Apparently, for such economists as Summers, language is nothing but a means of information gathering. In the United States as in Britain, linguistic competence is seen as a sign of particularly high education, but any Tunisian apprentice knows more languages than Larry Summers. A German secretary may well decide that she liked her holiday in Greece so much that she wants to learn the language, and take night courses between her (now annual) trips to Crete. Do they travel better? Certainly more thoroughly – and in some ways, more comfortably. Simply moving from one place to another in the care of a guardian – be it a college administrator, a distinguished conference organizer or a high-priced tour operator – contributes very little to coming of age, and it may even detract from it by giving us the illusion of having seen the world without ever having been in it. If you don't get your feet wet and your hands dirty you might as well stay home. You'll be able to see the Sistine Chapel better on the web anyway.

I will argue that the right kind of travel is indeed a crucial part of reaching maturity, though it is neither necessary nor sufficient for it. As de Beauvoir noted, seeing the world is not enough to make you content with your place in it. Nor need we travel in order to learn, formally, that different cultures have different ways. All you have to do is read the Bible to know that child sacrifice was part of many religions until God told Abraham he needn't do it, and what sixteen-year-old hasn't heard that the Eskimos let their elderly drift off on the ice floes? It may be an example that particularly appeals to teenagers, who are happy to use it as a piece of an argument for ethical relativism. But the engagement with another culture which real travel involves heightens our awareness of commonalities as well as differences. The commonalities as well as the differences will be subtler than you think, even in the case of cultures that speak (mostly) the same languages. Americans may be as captivated by *Downton Abbey* as the British are by Lady Gaga, but in the United States things like health care and maternity leave are called benefits, while in Britain, as in most of the civilized world, they are regarded as rights. Those words can make a world of difference in how you view justice and freedom.

As Kant said, it only makes sense to travel in other cultures if you've already made some sense of your own – though doing the former will certainly help you with the latter, for it allows you to notice the things in your own culture you once took for granted. When I returned to the States after my first six-year sojourn in Berlin I was outraged every time I opened the *New York Times*. This wasn't a matter of the content of its reporting but its form. While German papers print texts, and sometimes photographs illustrating them, the best available American newspaper thinks nothing of using three-quarters of a page for an advertisement and leaving the rest for the news. We do not think about the ways in which this shifts our attention from the slaughter in Bosnia to the sale at Bloomingdale's, but it does: when we see these spatial relations every morning, which event will seem larger? My attempt to make use of my outrage by weaving the example into the political philosophy classes I was teaching at Yale lasted a few months, maybe a year.

After a time I became so used to the paper again that my reactions to it were no longer visceral. Outrage is enervating, hence hard to retain very long.

This example is, of course, only a small instance of the ways in which we grow into societies that frame our perceptions of the world in ways we barely notice. It may not be an accident that *Peter Pan* was published shortly before the First World War. It would be foolish to say that J. M. Barrie knew what was coming, and A. S. Byatt's *The Children's Book* gives us a good look at what was going on behind the prettiest of games in what seems to us, nowadays, an innocent world. Still, compared to what came afterwards, the turn of the last century can seem so sweet we might wish time had stopped right there. But forget, if you can, the two world wars and the atom bomb that succeeded it, and consider the mid-century criticisms of Paul Goodman's classic, *Growing Up Absurd*. Have we created a culture that leaves space for grown-ups, a culture that makes growing up a good option? Goodman argued we have not. He believed that people need to grow into a culture that offers meaningful work, a sense of community and faith that the world is responsive to their efforts. When consuming goods rather than working becomes the focus of our culture, we have created (or acquiesced in) a society of permanent adolescents. Goodman's work, though enormously influential in the 1960s – Susan Sontag called him the American Sartre – has been largely forgotten, but much of his critique rings even truer today than it did fifty years ago. Even more can be said of the man whose vision of growing up most inspired Immanuel Kant – the fascinating and maddening Jean-Jacques Rousseau. Rousseau's work is a stinging indictment of the way in which culture merely 'weaves garlands of flowers around the chains that bind us'. Arts and sciences are more likely to serve our vanity, and our purses, than our common humanity; thus culture warps us into accepting a social order it ought to call into question. The allures of society are so seductive and pervasive that only radical solutions will do. The problems and promise of Rousseau's *Emile* – philosophy's only full-length attempt at a manual for coming of age – will be examined later in some detail. I will show how Rousseau and Kant set the terms of discussion, before exploring what makes growing up even harder in the twenty-first century.

Having failed to create societies that our young want to grow into, we idealize the stages of youth. Watching the wide-eyed excitement with which babies face every piece of the world, we envy their openness and naivety, while forgetting the fear and frustration that accompany every bit of progress, from standing upright to drawing a stick-figure. The most pernicious bit of idealization is the very widespread view that the best time of one's life is the decade between sixteen and twenty-six, when young men's muscles and young women's skin are at their most blooming. That's due to hormones, and evolutionary biologists will explain that it happens for a reason. But *your* goal is not to maximize reproduction, whatever may be said of your genes. By describing what is usually the hardest time of one's life as the best one, we make that time harder for those who are going through it. (*If I'm torn and frightened now, what can I expect of the times of my life that, they all tell me, will only get worse?*) And that is the point. By describing life as a downhill process, we prepare young people to expect – and demand – very little from it.

Few things show this better than the progressive transformation of the Peter Pan story. In the original novel, grown-ups are simply dull: Mr Darling's knowledge is confined to stocks and shares; his only passion is being exactly like his neighbours. By the mid-twentieth century the character is slightly menacing, an authoritarian who could become a tyrant so easily that the same actor could play father and pirate. By the end of the twentieth century, the grown-up had become ridiculous. In *Hook*, Steven Spielberg's disturbing twist on the story, Peter Banning is an object of contempt. Grown-ups are still boring and rigid, but they are now so pitiful that teenagers are right to mock them. The variations on the story reflect the decline of the image of adulthood itself. At the beginning of the twentieth century, growing up looked merely dreary; by the end it looked positively pathetic.

This book will discuss the ways in which our understanding of the way the world is, and the way it should be, are furthered – and hindered – by different kinds of experience. It will argue that being grown-up is itself an ideal: one that is rarely achieved in its entirety, but all the more worth striving for.

1. Historical Backgrounds

Possible Worlds

It's fair to ask whether philosophy can say much at all about a process as diverse as coming of age. Philosophers trade in general truths – some still seek necessary or universal ones – but even a little empirical data reveals that growing up is very particular. Coming of age in Samoa is not the same as coming of age in Southampton, and even within a single culture, decades can make a difference, and centuries can make the terrain look unrecognizable. French historian Philippe Ariès argued that early medieval Europeans had no concept of childhood; not until the twelfth century were children considered notable enough to be portrayed in paintings, and even then they were simply depicted as smaller-sized adults, with no difference of feature or expression. Later historians criticized Ariès for drawing too quick a conclusion from iconography to concepts, but his most important insight still stands: whatever concept of childhood medieval Europeans had, it wasn't ours. If we focus on images we can even ask if Ariès's concept of childhood is the same as the one we have today. When he wrote his seminal

Centuries of Childhood in 1960, could he have imagined the ease with which some of us take and share reams of baby videos that, apart from a limited number of social scientists, can only be of interest to the baby's grandparents and future fiancée?

Something surely changed when this became possible, but nothing as dramatic as the changes in thinking about childhood when people began to take for granted that their children would survive infancy. Seventeenth-century French children were as familiar with birth and death as they were with sex, and not merely in peasant dwellings where life, of necessity, took place in one room. The royal physician Héroard's diary contains observations like this one, recorded when the future Louis XIII was one year old: 'He laughed uproariously when his nanny waggled his cock with her fingers, an amusing trick which the child soon copied. Calling a page he shouted "Hey there!" and pulled up his robe, showing him his cock . . . in high spirits, he made everybody kiss his cock' (*Centuries of Childhood*, p. 100).

In our current rush to compensate for decades when sexual abuse was ignored, we'd do well to remember that not every form of attention to children's sexuality is an abuse of it. In early modern France, this sort of behaviour was considered perfectly normal until the age of seven or eight, when children were expected to treat sexual matters with more modesty. It is so far from Victorian expectations of innocence, or our current heightened concern over sexual predators and pederasty, that it can well be asked whether having a child's body was the same in those three epochs.

Having a child's mind could not have been the same in a world that had yet to emphasize the importance of education, or separate children from adults in new institutions called schools. Most early medieval European children were absorbed into the world of adult labour as soon as they were old enough to sweep a workshop floor. The expectation that boys should be secluded from adults to enjoy or endure a process of instruction began in the seventeenth century, and created the modern idea that childhood is long. The childhood of girls and poor children continued to be shorter than that of those youths who were sent to school. Even for the latter, we must wonder about the commonalities of experience in an age where school-children were armed, and regularly mutinied against their teachers in incidents like the one at Die, France, in 1649:

> The logicians barricaded themselves inside the college, prevented the masters and the pupils of other classes from entering, fired pistol shots, fouled the rostra in the first and third classrooms, threw the benches in the second classroom out of the window, tore up the books, and finally climbed out of the window of the fourth classroom. (Ibid, p. 318)

Ariès tells us that the great school mutinies ended in the late seventeenth century in France, though they continued into the nineteenth century in England, where schoolboys who set fire to their desks and books and withdrew to an island had to be subdued by a company of soldiers. The concepts of childhood and youth were as different from our own as the concept of adulthood which was meant to follow them:

> To make a success of life was not to make a fortune or at least that was of secondary importance; it was above all to win a more honorable standing in a society whose members all saw one another, heard one another and met one another nearly every day. (Ibid, p. 376)

It's always possible to construct parallels – certain forms of Facebook behaviour come to mind – but even these few examples make plain how far early modern ideas of life cycles differ from those we now take for granted. Most notably, contemporary historians have argued that the very idea of childhood as happy is a modern one. Barring an occasional fond word for his mother, hardly a classical author from Greece to China left a record of his childhood as golden, or expressed nostalgia or yearning for it.[1] For the seventeenth-century French philosopher René Descartes, human unhappiness is due to the fact that we begin our lives as children.

22

On the other side of the world in more recent times, American anthropologist Margaret Mead's study of adolescent girls in Samoa showed they were having the time of their lives. Mead meant this quite literally. When she wrote *Coming of Age in Samoa*, the bulk of young children's time was consumed by the task of baby-minding. From the age of five or six, the Samoan girl was usually found with a baby on her hip; until the age of eight or nine boys too took some care of the younger children. For both sexes, baby-tending consisted largely in keeping the babies quiet when in adult earshot. As the children grew, 'A fire or a pipe to be kindled, a call for a drink, a lamp to be lit, the baby's cry, the errand of the capricious adult – these haunt them from morning to night' (*Coming of Age*, p. 21).

If Samoan families were smaller, Mead wrote, this would divide the population into two groups: the sheerly self-sacrificing and the tyrannically self-indulgent.

> But just as a child is getting old enough so that its willfulness is becoming unbearable, a younger one is saddled upon it, and the whole process is repeated again, each child being disciplined and socialized through responsibility for a still younger one. (Ibid, p. 19)

The introduction of government schooling has since created a complete reorganization of Samoan household structures, and it's easy to pity those children who, at the time of Mead's research, were unable to have the freedom from labour we regard as essential to having a childhood. Yet it's clear that Samoan children had something ours lacked: the experience of making meaningful contributions to a community. Our children play with dolls or toy tea sets in imitation of tasks they will undertake as adults; the Samoan girl who minded her little brother was performing a crucial function that allowed her mother to go reef-fishing or work the plantation in between intervals of pregnancy. Instead of the long empty space where responsibilities are few and meanings are preparatory – our children are judged according to their performance on tests meant to ready them for real tasks, but which often have no relation to them – Samoan children did things that mattered, and they knew it. Mead's claim that this gave their lives greater coherence than ours have should not be mistaken for an apology for the millions of children still forced to work, primarily in Asia and Africa, under horrendous conditions today, but it is a call to think carefully about what we take for granted.

After puberty, however, Samoan girls were freed from the more tedious forms of labour assigned to young children, and delayed the time until they faced the new responsibilities that marriage brought. They passed their time with light work like weaving baskets, and moonlight trysts with the youths who could successfully woo them. Since Samoan sexual prowess was bound up with knowing how to satisfy the maidens, those trysts were sweet, yet they seldom became tangled enough to cause the kind of pangs we know from (most of) our first loves. Sexual relationships were many and brief. For Samoans, *Romeo and Juliet* was funny. Mead was well aware that the Samoan culture she described lacked a dimension we would miss:

> Love and hate, jealousy and revenge, sorrow and bereavement, all are matters of weeks. From the first months of its life, when the child is handed carelessly from one woman's hands to another, the lesson is learned of not caring for one person greatly, not setting up high hopes on any one relationship. (Ibid, p. 138)

Still she was adamant in underlining the ways in which that culture avoided the crises and conflicts we have come to view as natural to the transition from childhood to maturity. The Samoan adolescent was free to explore her body's desires at the moment they became urgent; should she disagree with her parents, there was usually a nearby relative to whom she could carry her roll of mats and mosquito net. Samoan girls passed

> through the same process of physical development through which our girls go, cutting their first teeth

and losing them, cutting their second teeth, growing tall and ungainly, reaching puberty with their first menstruation, gradually reaching physical maturity and becoming ready to produce the next generation. (Ibid, p. 135)

Yet none of this physical development was accompanied by the intellectual and emotional development we have come to view as quintessentially adolescent: the storms of disappointment and the strains of anticipation, the teetering between high idealism and sceptical scorn, the desperate, often helpless self-assertion in the search for a self of one's own.

Since Mead's book was even more of a twentieth-century classic than Ariès's, it was, like Ariès's, subject to professional scrutiny, some of which turned up misinterpretation and error. That's the nature of the empirical: you can get it wrong. Yet whatever misinterpretations they contained, both books remain important and enlightening, for both contain deeper truths that can be called philosophical. Childhood is not fixed, nor are the stages of life that follow it. And this truth is not merely a matter of historical or ethnological interest, for if our paths are not determined, then we are free to choose among them. At least in principle.

These sketches of two famous accounts of childhood and adolescence should remind us how different coming of age can be in different places and eras. Even small variations in space or time can produce worlds of difference. The first years of the Soviet Union, for example, saw experiments in progressive education that American philosopher John Dewey found enviable, while a child born just ten years later would experience the rigid authoritarian climate that Stalinism brought to schools as to other Russian institutions.[2] Even in relatively similar societies, differences in childhood assumptions can be vast, as I discovered on overhearing a conversation between my seven-year-old twin daughters in 1998. We were living in Tel Aviv at the time, and I no longer recall which of them first heard the disappointing news that their Massachusetts cousin would not be coming for a long-planned visit, and ran to tell her sister. The State Department had issued a warning against travelling to Israel, and my sister-in-law had put her foot down.

'What's the matter?' asked the daughter who'd just been informed. 'Is he sick?'

'He's fine,' said her sister. 'It has something to do with Saddam Hussein.'

'What's Saddam Hussein got to do with it?'

'I'm not sure,' the other reflected. 'I think they're not so used to wars in America. Maybe he doesn't have his own gas mask.'

'Don't be silly,' came the haughty answer. 'Everyone in the world has his own gas mask.'

Philosophy's greatest task is to enlarge our sense of possibility. When seeking examples to show the possibility of other lives or concepts than the ones we take for granted, many twentieth-century philosophers turned to science fiction. They might have done better to look to history or anthropology. As the examples I've just sketched make clear, so much more is possible than the world that we know. *That* insight is a philosophical one, and like most genuinely philosophical insights its undertone is normative, that is, a claim about how things ought to be. Philosophy can and should draw on the knowledge that can only be gained by looking at the world as it is and as it was, but its sights are always set on the world as it should be. This is what Kant meant when he wrote that the practical is primary. In one of the few autobiographical notes he left us, he explains how he came to that view:

> I am by nature an inquirer. I feel the consuming thirst for knowledge, the restless passion to advance ever further, the delights of discovery. There was a time when I believed that this is what confers real dignity upon human life, and I despised the common people who knew nothing. Rousseau set me right. This imagined advantage vanishes, and I learned to honor human nature. I should regard myself to be far more useless than a common laborer, if I did not believe that my work would contribute to restoring the rights of humanity.[3]

But given the varieties of the experiences of coming of age that the sketches above merely hint at, what general claims can philosophy make?

What Is *Enlightenment?*

Coming of age is an Enlightenment problem, and nothing shows so clearly that we are the Enlightenment's heirs, whether we acknowledge that heritage or not. In the fifth century B.C.E. Plato wrote at length about child-rearing; his *Republic* is studded with discussions of matters from the proper age for learning to play the flute to which tunes should be heard. Not until Rousseau would another philosopher turn his attention to such details. But Plato's attention to detail is not for the sake of the child or the adult she will become; his concern is more for the care and development of the state than of the individuals within it. In an age where traditional social roles began to loosen, the Enlightenment could begin to care about individual human development for its own sake – though political concerns were never very far in the background. Where traditional structures leave little room for deviation, it is no surprise that the Roman philosopher Cicero could describe the business of philosophy as learning how to die, one part of living that allowed for major variation. Once these structures were weakened, so that the course of coming of age was no longer straightforward, the right form of human development became a philosophical problem, incorporating both psychological and political questions and giving them a normative thrust. Thus enough basic features of growing up are common to modern Western societies – which are, for better and worse, increasingly models for growing up anywhere – for some general philosophical claims to make sense.

Kant would *define* Enlightenment as coming of age, so it would seem natural for him to write, in the 1786 essay 'Conjectural Beginning of Human History', that the first step of human reason is the realization that human beings have the capacity to choose their life's journey, unlike other animals, which are bound to just one. It's a capacity that loomed especially large to a man of the Enlightenment. Medieval French craftsmen or Polynesian chiefs had more choices to make about their lives than their horses or pigs did, but for the greater part of human history, individual choices about the paths a life could take were relatively few. Kant's world was just beginning to accept the open-endedness we take for granted, and he took every advantage of it. Had he been born a couple of generations earlier, the likelihood that the son of a barely literate saddle-maker would become a professor – not to mention one recognized in his lifetime as a major thinker – would have been virtually nil. It is still far more true than it should be that even in countries that claim to promote equality of opportunity, what your parents do influences the number of choices you will be able to make in your life. Still, compared to premodern societies, your life may be statistically, but not *inevitably* determined by your position as an infant. (The odd exceptions are notably anachronistic: the few remaining members of royalty. Prince George has no career choices.)

The choices we must make require more experience and better judgement at the crucial junctures where we need them most. For a very long time, others must make them for us: unlike other animals, human beings need education. Kant makes an exception for songbirds that, he says, are taught to sing by their mothers like children in school. Anyone who believes they learn to sing by instinct should, he suggests, put sparrows' eggs in a canary's nest and watch the baby sparrows learn to sing like their adoptive mother. Contemporary biologists have confirmed this.[4] But we aspire to be more than one-hit wonders, so there's more to be learned than singing a tune. Indeed, says Kant, 'the human being can only become human through education'. But what about the educators? Even those with the best of intentions are themselves in part the product of choices others made. Moreover, education should be education for a future we can only partly foresee. Leave aside technological progress: if we have any hope for moral progress, we want the next generation to be better than we are. A version of that wish is expressed in a popular Israeli song that sighs, 'Take care of the world, child / For we didn't manage to do it.' But one need not be so morose – or irresponsible – in hoping the next generation will become both wiser and braver than ours. Yet how can we possibly help to fashion capacities that are better than those we possess ourselves, even if we want to? No wonder Kant's *Lectures on Pedagogy* called education 'the greatest and most difficult problem that the human being can be given'.

Matters look even worse when we consider how often the best of intentions are missing. I've been taking the perspective of the benevolent parent or the dedicated teacher, but those are hardly the only ones who determine how education proceeds. As Kant often reminds us, governments prefer immature subjects to independent citizens. Contemporary expressions of that preference range from the growing practice of keeping us all under electronic surveillance, or industry's ability to keep us dazzled by a bewildering number of choices of automobiles or breakfast cereal – while keeping the far more important choices out of our hands. In most cases, the immaturity that governments desire need not be achieved by force or stealth, for we willingly collude in it. It is easier, after all, to let others do our thinking for us than to think for ourselves. Totalitarian regimes are seldom necessary and often counterproductive, for wherever the mechanisms of control are clearly present, some bold souls will be moved to contest them. Sooner or later, direct control leads to rebellion; indirect control leads to dependency. Simpler and subtler are the infantilizing processes of non-totalitarian societies that encourage our natural laziness by giving us comfort through a range of toys. Of course, neither smartphones nor automobiles are *described* as toys; crucially, they are portrayed as the tools without which no adult life is complete. By contrast, ideas of a more just and humane world are portrayed as childish dreams to be discarded in favour of the real business of acquiring toys, i.e., finding a steady job that fixes our place in the consumer economy. It's a perfidious reversal that leaves us permanently confused. No wonder Kant calls the exit from self-incurred immaturity the most important revolution that can occur within the human being.[5]

Let me summarize the problem Kant viewed as humankind's most important. We are born into a journey whose path is open, but whose contours ought to be self-evident. As our bodies and minds grow we are able to master them, and with them the world, in a series of stages that looks biologically and psychologically straightforward. It ought to be easy: we begin more helpless than the members of other species, gradually coming alive to the world and our place in it, increasingly gaining independence and experience till we become the self-determining adults our nature suggests we should be. But our own worst instincts, and a range of social forces, are all arrayed against it. Our own worst instincts: passivity is comfortable. Earlier ages minced no words and called us lazy; David Hume thought the majority of the world's evils could be cured if human beings were born a little more industrious. A range of social forces: even the best of governments will find it easier to rule immature and passive subjects than active citizens. Call this an institutional kind of laziness, writ large.

Post-Enlightenment people will not be content without *some* form of activity that expresses the desire to choose our life's journeys, and the neo-liberal way of fulfilling that need is far more effective than anything totalitarian regimes ever devised. We are kept dazzled by a wealth of small decisions; Steve Jobs revealed that the question of which washing machine to purchase could dominate his family's dinner table for weeks. (Nor did the brilliant inventor find this fact problematic; he offered it as an example of democratic deliberation.) Our opportunities for decision-making utterly exhausted, we ignore the fact that the important decisions are made by others we cannot even name. Or did you choose a world in which oil companies profit from wrecking the planet? Women are stoned for adultery or murdered for going to school? Children die of easily preventable diseases or are collaterally damaged by drones? Do your choices make a difference to any of these?

Only free and equal grown-ups can build a free and equal society, but if society has an interest in cultivating mindless dependents, where are the grown-ups to come from? *Which came first: the chicken or the egg?* is a children's conundrum, but behind it lies the most serious riddle in political philosophy. You can't get the one without the other, so how can we ever begin? These were the questions that tormented Jean-Jacques Rousseau, the first philosopher to treat growing up as the philosophical problem it is, and the only one to propose a comprehensive and radical solution. After nearly a decade of agonizing over the problem, and driving most of his friends away in the process, Rousseau offered an answer: we must radically reconsider the way we raise children. We should raise the child apart from society, creating for him a little one in which *everything makes sense.* A child raised properly will come of age slowly and surely to become a self-determining adult who can create, on a larger scale, a world that makes sense.

Two events were said to have shaken Kant so profoundly that he departed from his infamous routine and forgot to take his daily walk. (The routine makes for easy snickering, but how many of us slot a morning run or a yoga session into our day, knowing that if we don't make a regular appointment with our bodies we are likely to neglect them?) The second event was not surprising: the news of the French Revolution so thrilled the democrat Kant that it crowded every other interest out. A few years later, in the middle of the Terror, he would write that the natural excitement which uninvolved bystanders felt at the thought of the Revolution was proof of humankind's capacity to make moral progress. Most of us can understand how the sound of a distant revolution might disrupt our routine; three German newspapers quoted Kant on that score at the start of the Arab Spring. But the first event that interfered with Kant's walk is far less intuitive: Jean-Jacques Rousseau left him spellbound. It wasn't an easy experience. Kant later wrote that he had to read Rousseau's sentences several times in order to understand them, so stirred was he by the beauty of their prose. The experience was liberating, as we saw in the note that said it was Rousseau who changed his life and taught him his true calling. He also called Rousseau the Newton of the mind, the highest form of praise the eighteenth century could muster. Though many readers mistook Rousseau's critique as a call for Romanticism, Kant's reading of his work places him squarely in the Enlightenment.

On the surface, the only thing the two men had in common was class background. Rousseau's father made watches, while Kant's father made saddles, which put each boy squarely in the class of small artisans who could not have expected to receive much by way of an education, let alone become a major force of Western thought. Surely a strong sense of the effort required to become independently thinking adults made each of them view growing up as an ideal, not as a given. Coming of age at a time when even the contributors to the *Encyclopedia* – avowed engine, and product, of Enlightenment – could be offended by its editor Diderot's proposal to print their names without their titles, meant living in a world of class distinctions that were barely touched until the French Revolution. Rousseau always noticed, and commented on them keenly.

Still in every other way Kant and Rousseau seem different souls. Kant's routine was so regular his townsfolk set their watches by it; Rousseau threw away his own watch and was pleased to record the feeling of liberation that accompanied the act. Rousseau turned down a lifelong pension from the king of France to live the life of a (usually well-kept) vagabond; Kant became a Prussian professor. Rousseau's *Confessions* was the first work of modern autobiography, and he often lets allusions to his own life intrude into places in his works you may think they had no business; with the exception of the comment that residence in Königsberg can be a substitute for travelling, Kant's personal references are confined to a couple of unpublished notes. Rousseau's erotic life, both in fantasy and reality, was as intense, varied and open as many today; the only suggestion of Immanuel Kant as a sexual being is a letter from a local matron asking him to wind up her clock. The reference is to the opening of *Tristram Shandy*, whose hero was conceived during the monthly household clock-winding, but there it is, that clock again. Rousseau's travels were extraordinary even for his time, for he was no tourist: sometimes from choice, sometimes from necessity, he changed countries often. Though he never fit into any of them, it wasn't for want of trying.

He began as a fifteen-year-old apprentice who left his native Geneva to cross the Alps on foot into Italy, where he worked as a sign painter and engraver before getting a post as a diplomat's secretary. Moving to France, he styled himself as 'Mr Greene from England', earning a living giving music lessons though he'd never received any of his own. Nevertheless his first opera, *Le Devin du Village*, made such an impression on Louis XV that he was offered the post of royal composer, a post he turned down in order to live, more or less independently, as a writer who alternately enchanted and outraged the salons of Paris, and went off to the countryside to escape them. Several of his travels were involuntary, such as the one from France to Switzerland after being warned that his *Emile* was about to be burned by the public executioner in Paris, and advised to flee lest he meet a similar fate himself. There was also the ill-starred voyage to England as a guest of David Hume after the Swiss decided their native son was too wild after all, and the return to France after it proved clear David Hume was not his cup of tea. And these are only the highlights: his journeys were so many that a very careful reading of the *Confessions* is required to keep track of them. Kant, as we know, never left his native town.

Yet Rousseau was Kant's guiding star, and his Königsberg house contained one piece of art: a portrait of the wild Swiss philosopher. Much as Newton's *Principia* is the background text for most everything Kant wrote about nature, Rousseau's *Emile* is the text Kant took for granted in most everything he wrote about humankind. Although, as I will argue, it is fatally flawed, Rousseau's attempt to solve the problem is so important that it deserves its own discussion below.

Before turning to it, however, it's worth addressing the question: why turn to the Enlightenment at all? Enlightenment-bashing has become such a popular sport that it's hard to count the number of charges made against it. Here I will discuss only three.[6] The Enlightenment is often dismissed as Eurocentric. In fact it was the first modern movement to attack Eurocentrism and racism, often at considerable risk. Today Christian Wolff's name is known only to scholars, but in the early eighteenth century he was the most famous philosopher in Germany, and a major influence on the young Immanuel Kant. Yet in 1723 he was given forty-eight hours' notice to vacate his professorship at Halle, and the territory of Prussia, or face execution. His crime? Wolff had publicly argued that although the Chinese were a people without Christianity, they were a people with morals. Wolff's experience was not exceptional: nearly all the canonical Enlightenment texts were burned, banned or published anonymously. For however different they were, all seemed to threaten established authority in the name of universal principles available to anyone, whether Christian or Confucian, Persian or French. To be sure, offensive remarks about Jews or Africans can be found in many an Enlightenment correspondence, or even a publication. Such remarks are often emphasized today, while passages like Kant's attack on colonialism are overlooked:

> Compare the inhospitable actions of the civilized and especially of the commercial states of our part of the world. The injustice which they show to lands and peoples they visit (which is equivalent to conquering them) is carried by them to terrifying lengths. America, the lands inhabited by the Negro, the Spice Islands, the Cape, etc., were at the time of their discovery considered by these civilized intruders as lands without owners, for they counted the inhabitants as nothing . . . [they] oppress the natives, excited widespread wars among the various states, spread famine, rebellion, perfidy, and the whole litany of evils which afflict mankind. China and Japan, who have had experience with such guests, have wisely refused them entry. (Kant, *Perpetual Peace*, 1795, Third Article)

Anyone who praises China and Japan for keeping out predatory Europeans cannot fairly be accused of blindly imposing Western ways on the rest of the world. Enlightenment thinkers were men of their time, educated by men of earlier ones, and their struggle to free themselves of prejudice and preconception could never be final. But it is fatal to forget that those thinkers were not only the first to condemn Eurocentrism and racism; they also laid the theoretical foundation for the universalism upon which all struggles against racism must stand.

It's also common to attack the Enlightenment for its elevation of human reason. The Enlightenment in general, and its greatest philosopher, Kant, in particular, are accused of holding reason in the sort of uncritical adulation earlier ages had for God. The frequency of the charge is puzzling in view of the fact that you needn't read much to see its foolishness – the very first sentence of the *Critique of Pure Reason* is a statement about reason's limits. Enlightenment thinkers never held reason to be unlimited; they just refused to let church and state be the ones to set the limits on what we can think. Nor is reason opposed to passion, a subject to which Enlightenment thinkers devoted nearly as much space as to thought. This was an age, after all, in which men and women wept in public over melodrama. For calling reason our highest faculty, Kant has been compared to the Reign of Terror and the Marquis de Sade, or less dramatically dismissed as dour, severe and slightly mad. Readers who do so misunderstand his conception of reason entirely. It's a large conception, embracing the capacity to do logic and mathematics and figure out the best means to getting whatever end you may happen to want tomorrow. But these, for Kant, are banal sorts of reasoning. Far more important is what he calls the real use of reason: the ability to form ideas of goodness, truth and beauty that orient us in action. Through those ideas, reason can make claims on nature and validate thereby our deepest longings. *Pace* fashionable caricatures, the Enlightenment's icon is not the cold, rule-obsessed technocrat but Mozart's self-possessed Figaro – the servant who uses his own reason to get the better of his feudal master in order to realize the passion that is deeper and truer than any the aristocracy can display.

Finally, and most recently, it's common to blame the Enlightenment for ecological disaster. Critics charge that Enlightenment thinkers' inclination to defend what they considered reasonable over what was considered natural set up an opposition between reason and nature which encouraged the human domination of nature that has so dramatically backfired in recent years. This objection ignores the fact that the Enlightenment appealed to nature more often than not, arguing that the claims of reason were more natural than the claims of arbitrary convention. Even more important, where reason was opposed to nature, it was in the interest of questioning conventions that tradition insisted were natural. Consider some of the things generally held to be natural at the start of the eighteenth century: poverty, slavery, the subjection of women, feudal hierarchies and most forms of illness. As late as the nineteenth century some English clerics would argue that efforts to relieve the Irish famine contravened the natural order willed by God. What is natural is contested. As Enlightenment thinkers realized, you cannot abolish slavery, overthrow existing hierarchies or cure illness unless you can show that they are not necessarily part of the way the world is. The ability to question what is natural and what is not is the first step towards any form of progress. The Enlightenment sought moral progress; technological progress was only desirable insofar as it brought humankind more happiness and freedom. To be sure, it was impossible to foresee every consequence of the technological advances the Enlightenment set in motion. But before you blame the Enlightenment for some of the technological advances we might do without, you might pause to be grateful for the processes it set in motion that doubled the lifetime you have in which to complain about it.

Why turn to the Enlightenment? There is no better option. Rejections of the Enlightenment result in premodern nostalgia or postmodern suspicion; where Enlightenment is at issue, modernity is at stake. A defence of the Enlightenment is a defence of the modern world, along with all its possibilities for self-criticism and transformation. If you're committed to Enlightenment, you're committed to understanding the world in order to improve it. Twenty-first-century Enlightenment must extend the work of the eighteenth by examining new dangers to freedom, and extending social justice. Growing up depends on both.

Breaking Chains

Rousseau describes the right path to adulthood against the norm he has in view:

> We were made to be men; laws and society have plunged us once more into childhood. The rich, the nobles, the kings are all children who, seeing that men are eager to relieve their misery, derive a puerile vanity from that very fact and are very proud of care that one would not give to them if they were grown men. (*Emile*, p. 85)

The information that Prince Charles has a servant to squeeze toothpaste onto his toothbrush can make one wonder how much has changed since Rousseau's lament, but few of us, honestly, really envy Prince Charles. The warning applies to those of us whose cages are more ample, and less gilded. Rousseau makes clear the multitude of ways that civilization infantilizes us. He held that all of us are born free, but are everywhere in chains. The famous sentence comes from his *Social Contract* (1764), but the note is sounded in the very first text he wrote. The *Discourse on the Arts and Sciences* (1749) challenged the Enlightenment's most basic assumption that culture and science are the only means to progress, and in particular to freedom. Not only, he wrote, do they not lead to progress; they actually enslave us. The tools they took for liberation turned out to be garlands of flowers that decorate – and conceal – the chains that bind us. 'Need raised up thrones; the arts and sciences made them strong.' Culture, as it stands, is less despotic but more powerful than government itself, making us love our own slavery by convincing us that this is what civilization comes to. Two passions, for glory and for luxury, are the source of all our ills; we are wicked because of the one and miserable because of the other.

Luxury corrupts everything: the rich who enjoy it as well as the wretched who covet it. Even worse, it turns human beings into market values, letting us appraise people like herds of cattle. Rousseau is no ascetic: many passages of the *Confessions* extol the pleasures of good wine, and *Emile*'s descriptions of the joys of fresh fruit can sound ecstatic. No particular trifle – be it good food or the latest hi-tech toy – is an evil in itself. The problem is that they create false needs that make us dependent. The pleasure you get from buying the latest smartphone is briefer than your anxiety and confusion when you forget to charge it: suddenly you are helpless. Even those of us who are slow to take up new bits of technological progress can hardly remember what life was like before them. Those who rule society promote our dependency; they do everything in their power to cultivate a taste for luxury, to deceive us into thinking that more luxury will make us feel sexy and satisfied. In doing so, they distract us from thinking about the real matters that condition our lives. You can walk into any electronics store and choose from a dizzying number of smartphones. How many choices can you make about the government that represents you, the use of tax moneys that it claims from you, the laws to which you are bound?

Minus the smartphone, this is all in Rousseau's first *Discourse*, which caused a sensation in Paris in 1750. Other philosophers had inveighed against luxury; Voltaire, for example, wrote that Satan's mistake was tempting Job with misery, for we're more likely to turn to religion when we are wretched than when we are very comfortable. It's a clever version of the claim that there are no atheists in foxholes. But this sort of criticism lacked the complexity of Rousseau's. It would take twentieth-century Marxists like Marcuse (and, less lucidly, Adorno and Horkheimer) to make such arguments again. When we take time to look at

46

them closely, they have lost none of their power. So far you might think they apply to Steve Jobs or Anna Wintour, but not to the creators of higher forms of culture. What about the writers and critics, artists and philosophers whose business is precisely to confront the things that really matter? According to Rousseau, we're the worst of the lot. First of all, we are no less susceptible to the temptations of luxury than anyone else is, and rather more susceptible to the temptations of vanity. So we construct the justifications that keep our careers, and the world as it is, going, weaving garlands of rationalization around the chains that bind us all. Those who raise concrete and serious doubts about them will seem self-righteous, preachy or just plain nuts.

Rousseau was accused of all three. Immediately recognized as brilliant, the *Discourse* turned the thirty-eight-year-old vagabond into a Paris sensation – until the denizens of the salons realized that he hadn't simply written the piece in order to win the first prize of the Academy of Dijon. He was entirely serious. The first *Discourse* was followed by a second, in which Rousseau argued that inequality and private property were the source of all our woes, and seemed to advocate a return to the state of nature. The fact that this attack on civilization came from a self-taught genius the Parisians had just condescended to patronize must have been particularly galling. Here's what Voltaire wrote as thanks for the copy of the second *Discourse* the younger man had sent him:

> I have received, Monsieur, your new book against mankind . . . Never has anyone used so much cleverness to make us into beasts. Reading your book makes one feel like marching on all fours. However, since I lost that habit more than sixty years ago, I unfortunately feel that it is impossible for me to regain it, and I leave that natural gait to those who are worthier of it than you or I. (Letter to Rousseau, 30 August 1755)

It's unlikely that Voltaire read the book with any care, and the same must be said of the many people who, to this day, follow him by repeating that Rousseau was calling for a return to a state of nature. He was not, though he thought the state of nature was better than the state we're in. Only a cursory reading of *Emile*, which he called his best and brightest book, could confirm the philosophers' suspicions. Rousseau's insistence that developing mature moral character requires forbidding the child access to both books and society demanded the child reject everything they had to offer. They should have read more carefully, for *Emile* is the clearest and most detailed practical manual of Enlightenment ever written. If Emile is to begin by remaining in ignorance, it's only the better to overcome it.

Emile purports to be a record of an experiment in raising an ordinary boy under conditions that will lead him to become a genuinely free adult. The experiment is all in Rousseau's head, but this will seem less preposterous when we learn that eighteenth-century chemistry, for example, was not conducted in laboratories, but by means of what was called rational analysis. Even in natural science, thought experiments were experiments like any other. In fact, *Emile* is a book without a genre. Its first sentence is a statement of theodicy – a defence of Creation and its Creator – its last is the happy end of a sentimental novel. In between is the first modern manual for child-raising, a sharp attack on the established church and a mixture of epistemological and political reflection. Its attention to our bodies is sharp and explicit, its flights into fantasy no less so. Before we can ask whether it belongs to the Enlightenment, shouldn't we ask whether it belongs to philosophy?

This is a book that raises questions about both. Neither the Enlightenment nor philosophy should look the same after you've finished it. The questions it raises will seem less strange if you place *Emile* by the side of the book Rousseau seldom forgot while writing it: Plato's *Republic*. *Emile* isn't odd if you remember that the very first book of Western philosophy similarly moves between fantasy and argument, interrupts itself with myth and non sequitur and puts discussions of the right sort of sexual relations, and the wrong sort of rhythm, in the middle of what is unmistakably metaphysics. Both turn to political theory, however, as a way of answering another question, which Kant would describe as the question of the systematic relation between happiness and virtue: shouldn't what you do in the world be related to what the world does to you? Living rightly with this question is the single most important task of becoming adult.

Emile was an attempt to provide the basis for healing the split between reason and nature that elsewhere gapes like an open wound. To see this, it's important to understand *Emile* not only as a piece of philosophy; unlike many seminal texts on education that built on it, it is also a demand for philosophy as, if done rightly, a part of being grown-up. For Rousseau, philosophy and Enlightenment are one enterprise, and it's intrinsically related to the subject of *Emile*: growing up properly. Much of *Emile*'s apparent peculiarity, even as a set of instructions for raising a child, is connected to the seriousness with which Rousseau takes the task Kant would go on to describe as thinking for yourself. Unlike the philosophers whose call to *écrasez l'infâme* masked a deep reliance on convention, Emile will be raised to have no habits. Thinking for himself in childhood is exercise for doing so as a man. Or to put it the other way round: the child who is surrounded by babbles of baby-talk, the schoolboy who is forced to sit still before a teacher's blather will not squirm when he hears a politician's empty lies. Because Rousseau knows how easy it is to refuse to think for yourself, his training can seem hard. His prescriptions are a curious mixture of infinite love and apparent brutality. This last, he insists, is only perceived as such by those who would prepare the child for a state of permanent infantilization. Here is his attack on the normal teacher:

> About what do you want him to think, when you think about everything for him? What need does he have to foresee rain? He knows that you look at the sky for him. What need has he to organize his walk? He has no fear that you would let the dinner hour pass. You may soften his body by inactivity, you do not for that make his understanding more flexible. On the contrary, *you complete the work of discrediting reason in his mind by making him use the little he possesses on the things which appear the most useless.* (*Emile*, p. 118, italics added)

Like reading and writing and arithmetic, none of which the child will learn until he is twelve, Rousseau's view of intellectual development rests on a belief, so evident from experience that it hardly needs to be confirmed by philosophers like John Locke, that the senses develop before reason in time. This gives them no particular authority over it; it's just a matter of chronology. It seems but good sense for Rousseau to describe childhood as 'reason's sleep' (p. 107). On these nearly trivial observations Rousseau built a theory of moral development which was largely confirmed by later psychologists. Children are not born acting on principle, and most adults never get there. If we want them to have a chance of doing so, we have to adopt an education appropriate to their development.

One way to bring home how radical this idea must have seemed is to take a look at portraits of children up to Rousseau's time. It needn't be Velásquez's portrait of a Spanish *infanta*; any child whose parents were noteworthy enough to get its portrait painted was dressed in the stiff and formal – albeit gorgeous – clothing that was a miniature version of what its parents wore. Rousseau's demand that children be given clothes that feel comfortable, and get dirty, may seem trivial in an age of designer jeans, but it was part of his insistence that childhood is not a faulty version of adulthood, but a form of life in its own right. All of us who wore overalls and sneakers and made mud-pies owe him a debt – as do those of us who were breast-fed, or nursed our own children. In Rousseau's day, women who could afford it left their babies to a wet nurse. His insistence that babies should be nursed by their mothers from the day they are born was taken up in Kant's lectures on education – a detail that shows us just how wide the scope of philosophy can be.

No books at all? Rousseau's attacks on culture come from an awareness of its power. He is brutally clear about the ways in which culture can enslave us. Let us count them: it can, if you're lucky, provide you with income; as long as the crowd is applauding, it can give you a tenuous sense of self-esteem; it may even provide you with moments so sublime that you're prepared to ignore more important, moral facets of the world in order to enjoy them. Only one so conscious of the force of culture can be conscious of its capacity to subdue us. Next to Rousseau's descriptions of the mechanisms by which culture holds us in bondage, the blithe Enlightenment assurance that culture is an instrument of liberation shows a superficial awareness of its claims. It's as if someone who'd written an essay in praise of love after a lifetime of light flirtation found himself confronted by a man with a broken heart. Just because Rousseau's awareness is as subtle as it is fervent, his attempts to free himself will verge on the tortured: 'I want nothing more to do with a deceitful profession in which one believes one is doing much for wisdom while doing everything for vanity.'[7] After reading Rousseau's critique of philosophy, anyone who hasn't occasionally felt the force of such an outburst is either a saint or a liar.

How does a man with this sense of vulnerability approach the task of educating a child to adulthood?

The young Emile will be allowed no books, not because Rousseau despises them but because he adores them. Emile learns those things that naturally spark his interest – not the rote lessons that were enforced by corporal punishment, or more subtly, by the wish to show off to his elders. His astronomy lesson takes place in the forest, where his tutor has taken him at twilight; Emile is hungry, and needs to learn the position of the stars to guide his way back home. He learns mathematics by figuring out what angle the ladder must be placed to pick the cherries, what height the rope must be to place a swing. Every step in an education for freedom should be freely chosen. At the age of ten, Emile 'does not know what routine, custom or habit is. What he did yesterday does not influence what he does today. He never follows a formula, does not give way before authority or example, and speaks only as it suits him' (*Emile*, p. 160).

The most important thing he learns is to respect the limits provided by the natural world – and nothing else. Children should yield to the forces of nature, but never to the commands of other people. Rousseau thinks that common treatment of crying babies fosters both the false needs and subordination he is determined to prevent. The crying baby, he tells us, soon learns that after his initial true needs for food and warmth are satisfied, he can continue to cry and thereby control the wills of all the adults around him.

If we allow him to do so, he soon learns that control over people's wills is more valuable than control or adaptation to things. And this means that his first ideas are those of domination and submission. It also leads to superstition, for the child attributes will to natural objects, and the world as a whole. So Rousseau tells us to let the child wail, for 'it is important to accustom him early not to give orders either to men, for he is not their master, nor to things, for they do not hear him'. He then turns to example to show that children do not perceive natural suffering as unjust, or natural limits as constraints. 'The cookies are all gone' produces a very different reaction than 'You can't have one before dinner'. If the child is to be educated for freedom, he must be educated to submit to nothing but the demands of nature. If he breaks a window, his punishment is not chastisement; he will simply have to sleep in the cold.

Rousseau's claim, in his *Social Contract*, that 'men must be forced to be free' should seem less ominous in light of his analysis of the ways in which we – with society's blessing – contribute to our own enslavement. Still critics have complained that Emile's freedom is illusory, for he is accompanied day and night by an all-seeing tutor who is able to manipulate the environment so as to make all causes and effects appear natural. But how do you educate a child to be free? Freedom isn't merely licence; Rousseau and

Kant tell us it's the capacity to obey a law that you give to yourself. Freedom cannot simply mean doing whatever strikes you at the moment; that way you're a slave to any whim or passing fancy. Real freedom involves control over your life as a whole, learning to make plans and promises and decisions, to take responsibility for your actions' consequences. How is the child to learn this if, like Peter Pan, he is ruled by the successive play of desires? How then to develop a self that will be capable of freedom?

Remember: a free child submits only to the necessity of things, not to other people's wills. So he cannot be given commandments, even by the best of tutors or parents. However eminently reasonable they may be, the child will perceive them as the arbitrary expression of another will. The tutor, therefore, must manipulate the appearance of natural necessity, determining Emile's will without creating resentment. By doing so he fosters Emile's feeling of satisfying his own desires, so he experiences doing what pleases him for his own reasons and with his own strength. This gives Emile a taste of what it's like to be free: neither a slave to his own whims nor to the will of others. We can call it managed freedom: extending Emile's experience of freedom by letting him learn self-reliance through pleasure, while controlling the environment so that nothing goes wrong.

Among the many bits of apparently random advice contained in *Emile* is this one:

Many night games. This advice is more important than it seems. Night naturally frightens men and sometimes animals as well ... I have seen reasoners, strong-minded men, philosophers, soldiers intrepid by daylight tremble like women at the sound of a leaf in the night. This fright is attributed to the tales of nurses. It has a natural cause ... the same one which makes men distrustful and people superstitious: ignorance of the things which surround us and of what is going on about us. (*Emile*, p. 134)

Unlike the strong-minded men and philosophers whom Rousseau can't resist taking another shot at, Emile will never be prey to superstition, nor afraid of the dark. As Rousseau lays out ways in which the most ordinary practices should be arranged so as to leave us immune to any but natural authority, he is filling in the spaces that other Enlightenment thinkers simply left as empty wishes. The metaphor of light and darkness to express what we mean when we oppose reason to superstition has seemed so natural that it goes all the way back to Akhenaten, the Egyptian pharaoh who preceded Moses in establishing monotheism, and the words for 'light' and 'clarity' are built into every European word for 'Enlightenment' itself.

Simple lout that he was, Rousseau took his metaphors seriously. They wanted to bring light to humankind? Rousseau has his child roam fearless in the night. So it was with other forms of democratic ideals. Far closer to the working classes than were his critics, he was far more willing to let them in on Enlightenment too. Few were as explicit as Hume in leaving the people to be governed by habits the enlightened few could leave behind, or as cynical as Voltaire in maintaining for the masses the very superstitions his writings were devoted to undermining. But most tacitly accepted the assumption that Enlightenment would be restricted to the bourgeoisie, with varying degrees of bad conscience. With Rousseau, it is different, for the point of *Emile* is to show that any ordinary boy can grow up to live the Enlightenment dream: of not only becoming a man whose freedom is second to none, but also one who, at the end, is a philosopher.

Emile's education has made him free of the chains of state authority as well as the garlands that disguise them. As an adolescent, however, he will not only read books; he may go on to write them. Twice the book tells us that Emile, without knowing it, will become a philosopher, though 'if he writes books it will be not in order to pay court to the powers that be but to establish the rights of humanity' (p. 458). It seems certain that Kant took the hint; as we saw, he wrote that Rousseau changed his life by showing him that all his scholarship was of less value than the work of a common labourer, unless it helped to establish the rights of humanity.

Emile's slow introduction to culture is based not

merely on Rousseau's indignation at the rote learning to which children of his day were subject, nor on empirical observation of children's development, but also on the theory of humankind's development laid out in the *Discourse on Inequality* (1755). In Rousseau's version of human history, the savage lived in isolation until accidents of nature drove him to form rough group settlements. These might have remained benign had not culture and sexuality, born at the same moment, combined to lead us into a cycle of vanity that produced inequalities from which we never recovered. As Rousseau tells it, the desire to do more than simply copulate and reproduce like other species is the desire to *be desired* – the element of sexuality which is peculiarly human. That desire led primitive folk towards the first forms of culture, adorning themselves with paint and feathers, inventing song and dance to get the attention of the opposite sex. We were left not only with permanent rivalry, but the inability to see ourselves except as reflected in the eyes of others – two facts that poisoned most further attempts at civilization.

Culture and sexuality thus come from the same source, and each draws much of its power from the other. Emile will need no culture until he reaches puberty – and then he'll need it bad. At this point history and poetry can teach him what he now needs to know about the human heart and soul. For by turning a natural drive into a search for the ideal erotic object – a woman who is as good as she is beautiful – the educator can create a love for the ideal itself that produces forms of striving that will be of real value. If properly managed, sexual desire can be the natural connection between self-interest and morality.

Like many others, Rousseau sought the right sort of link between members of civil society. Hobbes's instrumentalist social contract presumes we can only be linked by fear – of each other, as well as of anarchy – while standard Enlightenment assumptions that we are naturally sociable presume too much. Rousseau held that we are naturally neither as bad nor as benevolent as his forebears assumed.[8] While we, like other animals, are inclined to compassion, our interest in our own freedom comes first. But there is one act in which your interest is naturally identical with the interest of another. Erotic love, at its best, dissolves the tension between human desires. Thus Rousseau thought that love between men and women could be the cornerstone on which a decent society might be founded. The theme is introduced just after his discussion of religion, which denied that grace – hence religious education – is required for salvation. No wonder church authorities thought the book should be burned. Instead of religion, Emile is prepared to find his salvation in love. To keep his erotic sights focused, the tutor describes an ideal girl called Sophie, and to make sure we get his message, Rousseau draws our attention to the fact that the name is not an accident. *Philo-sophia* means love of wisdom; Emile will find both at once.

By the end of the book Rousseau is so enthralled with his creation that he has switched to the first person: it's Jean-Jacques who is the perfect tutor who forced (prodded, guided) Emile to be free. The contemporary reader who may have followed Emile's and Jean-Jacques's journey towards adulthood is liable to be pulled up short in the final book – not because it has become a sentimental novel with a happy ending, but because it's an ending most of us will reject. Rousseau's discussion of the boy's education is as uncompromisingly radical as his discussion of the girl's is disappointing. He is to be raised without convention, she is to be raised to conform to most of them – because, says Rousseau, while a man should submit to none but natural authority, a woman should submit to a man's. Such a view was beginning to look reactionary in corners of the eighteenth century: the fact that Voltaire's beloved mistress, Madame du Châtelet, translated Newton and wrote treatises on physics was clearly one of her charms. And whatever he thought of Voltaire, we know Rousseau revered Plato, whose *Republic* claimed that men and women who were educated equally would have equal abilities, rights and duties. But Plato was a welcome anomaly in the history of philosophy; it would take more than two millennia until John Stuart Mill wrote a critique of sexism. I will not speculate about why Rousseau took such a step backwards, but I will claim that his miserable discussion of women's education does not threaten the core of his theory. It wouldn't be hard to rewrite the final book of *Emile*, making Sophie's education a counterpart to Emile's, and propose the love of these two free and equally unconventional persons to be the foundation of a free society. Alas, as we will see, Book V is not *Emile*'s only problem.

Important as *Emile* proved to be for the history of philosophy and education, it was immediately attacked. The church burned the book for its assault on religious education, but that was a last grasp of a dying ecclesiastical hold on political authority. The more interesting attacks on Rousseau were made by his erstwhile colleagues. These were mostly *ad hominem*, the sort of arguments about the man rather than his work that philosophers generally consider off-limits. But with a man whose work was so self-consciously personal, might they be legitimate? The search for sincerity and authenticity runs throughout Rousseau's work – whether he is debunking the self-deluded claims of high culture, or examining his own lapses and sins. If his own behaviour diverged so radically from the principles he so fervidly proclaims, shouldn't he be held to account?

It's a question Rousseau did his best to answer, at least in regard to his literary output: how can a man who declaims against the ill effects of culture continue to produce it? He avows his commitment to producing only such works as would avoid his own objections, that is, only those that help us to become better and freer. He even offers to burn his own work should his readers believe he has not met his own standard. He also points out that any criticism that his practice doesn't live up to his principles can only prove he's behaved badly, but doesn't reflect on the principles themselves. It is reason, he wrote, which shows us the goal, though passion may divert us from reaching it. With proper education, reason and passion work together, but few of us have the good fortune to be educated properly. Isn't that as true of the author of *Emile* as of anyone else? Few people in history have publicly admitted to more dubious behaviour, nor questioned their own motives in the search for sincerity. It's Rousseau himself, after all, who alerts us to the possibility that his refusal of the king's pension may have been more the result of his anxiety over the prospect of having to speak at court than of the nobler desire for independence. His pursuit of self-knowledge was extraordinary; it is fair to say he single-handedly invented the notion of bad faith, that peculiar form of self-deception later developed by the French existentialists.

But what if the behaviour in question is not simply continuing to create works of genius after winning fame for arguing that culture undermines morality, but abandoning five infants while writing a masterpiece about the importance of devoted child-raising? Even for those inclined to be indulgent towards human failings, this much of a gap between theory and practice will be hard to accept – particularly when they learn of the mortality rates in eighteenth-century French orphanages, where all five infants born to Rousseau's lifelong companion, the illiterate washerwoman Thérèse, were sent. Much later, Rousseau expressed regret about the fact that the conditions of his life did not permit him to raise children in the manner they deserved. It is true that his finances were precarious, and he was often on the run, whether because of quarrels he provoked or political persecution he endured. It was not an ideal framework for raising a child, much less for raising one with the superhuman devotion of Emile's guardian. Nevertheless: given that 80 percent of infants left in French orphanages were liable to die there, wouldn't an inferior upbringing have been a better choice?

There is no good way to square Rousseau's tenderness towards abstract children with the callousness with which he decided the fates of his own very real ones. Pointing out that almost none of the major figures in the history of philosophy, including Rousseau's critics, had any children at all may undermine, just a little, the authority of the critics, but it will do nothing to elevate Rousseau. It was he, after all, who insisted that fathers' responsibility for their children consists of a great deal more than conceiving and providing for them.

Was the man simply mad? It's a charge that was made often enough in his lifetime, and even more often thereafter. Jean Starobinski, who is both a psychoanalyst and one of Rousseau's greatest interpreters, wrote that the list of the diagnoses that have been made of Rousseau say more about the history of psychiatry than it does about the man. This is not the place to investigate them, but even without more biographical discussion, you may be struck by the depth of the paradox involved in realizing Rousseau's views, which is hardly ameliorated by the fact that he was the first to point to it. In the *Social Contract* he wrote a programme for 'men as they are, and laws as they should be'; in *Emile* he offered a strategy for creating men as they should be within laws as they are. Neither, it seems, could get off the ground without the other. If not mad in any other sense, didn't his work show him to be so out of touch with reality as to be considered, at the least, of unsound mind?

> 'Propose what can be done', they never stop repeating to me. It is as if I were told 'Propose doing what is done' or at least 'Propose some good which can be allied with the existing evil'. Such a project, in certain matters, is more chimerical than mine. For in this alliance the good is spoiled, and the evil is not cured.

I would prefer to follow the established practice in everything than to follow a good one halfway. There would be less contradiction in man. (*Emile*, p. 158)

So Rousseau anticipated our objections in the preface to *Emile*. Is it contradictory that a society in which individual freedom is cherished could also be one in which social bonds are most highly valued? A society in which people are tolerant of diversity and friendly to strangers, but willing to die as proud patriots for their country if necessary? Where life is frugal rather than luxurious, but given over to periodic rejoicing in great bacchanalian festivals? Where the ideal man is gentle, modest, lenient, but also heroic, courageous, strong-willed? Where love and sexuality combine not only to strengthen each other, but also the bonds of society itself? These are features of Rousseau's ideal society, in which all true human needs are satisfied. He was the first who dared to ask: what if we could have it all?

He was under no illusions about the difficulty of his project. 'I show the goal that must be set; I do not say that it can be reached. But I do say that he who comes nearest it will have succeeded best.' (*Emile*, p. 95.) He was also the first philosopher to ask whether the constraints that we take to be part of the human condition are in fact self-imposed. His answer to objections that his proposals go against human nature is as simple as it's true: 'We *do not know* what our nature

66

permits us to be!' We do not. Very deep assumptions about human nature have been overturned in the last fifty years; just think about the changes in Western views of gender or race or power. Rousseau overcame any number of supposedly natural constraints in his own lifetime, a time in which real restructuring of society, depending on restructuring assumptions about human nature, took place. We may be living in such a time again, if we stop focusing our attention on new forms of technological progress and allow Rousseau to help us think about other kinds of possibility.

It is never crazy to say that life contains more possibility than you have been told. What, then, can we say of the potential for achieving Rousseau's experiment? Emile's coming of age takes place under conditions that are almost impossible to organize. For a start, it requires the full-time commitment of a guardian for some twenty years. Even if you share Rousseau's view that no task in the world is more important than raising a child properly, you may have to earn a living; even if you needn't earn a living you might turn out to have twins. The attention the guardian is told to devote to the child is so complete that it precludes siblings, so even a return to traditional divisions of labour that left women in charge of child-rearing, should you choose it, would rarely be enough to fulfil Rousseau's programme. Emile is to be raised in the country, away from the seductions of society – difficult to arrange at a time when even remote bucolic villages are getting broadband. All these conditions were hard enough to fulfil in Rousseau's day, and may be even harder in ours, but they are not in principle impossible, just a matter of very complicated logistics. Reading the book can tempt you to undertake them, for the logic of *Emile* can seem necessary and compelling.

But logic, as Kant told us, is reason's least important achievement, and one aspect of Rousseau's proposal is, however, not logically but metaphysically impossible. The guardian's attention to Emile, more extensive than the most devoted parent can imagine, is not for the sake of Emile's safety or comfort. As Kant would later echo, Rousseau is adamant that a healthy number of bruises acquired by tumbling and falling is far better than the cosseting that prevents the child from standing on his own. The guardian's concern is not for Emile's physical but his moral safety. To ensure it, the guardian must completely control Emile's world. For the right kind of child-rearing requires that the world always make sense. Emile never experiences a gap between what is and what should be; virtue and happiness always go together. Each of his efforts is naturally rewarded: instead of empty marks or praise for memorizing geometric theorems, he gets the cherries on the tree when he figures out the proper angle for the ladder he needs to climb to them. What unhappiness occurs is the result of natural necessity; should he gorge himself on junk food, his belly will ache. Having been raised apart from servants or masters, he does not know haughtiness or obsequiousness, and meets the few people he does meet on equal terms, for he knows no other. Nothing ever seems to him unfair or arbitrary.

A child raised in this way would very likely be naturally moral, for he trusts the world to work as it should. Where it doesn't, the guardian steps in to discretely create the appearance of natural necessity, so that Emile will never perceive a gap between the *is* and the *ought*. But this ability, Kant will tell us, is available only to God, who (presumably) controls the entire natural world as He (presumably) sees into the depths of human hearts. The guardian is thus not only more patient, even-tempered and available than any guardian the world has known; he is qualitatively different from all of them, for he possesses the attributes monotheism assigns to God: omnipotence, omniscience and benevolence. Should Emile's world ever be out of joint, the guardian is always there to give it a nudge so that in Emile's own eyes, everything is as it should be.

But isn't it crazy to want to be God? This question should loom all the larger for the reader who is puzzled by the change in pronouns in the middle of *Emile*. Rousseau moves from describing the perfect guardian to becoming him, clearly carried away by the fantasy of controlling the world for the child he wished he had raised. Yet none other than the sane and sober Kant would tell us that the wish to be God is part of being human. The message of his metaphysics is to warn us against it; more precisely, to show us how the wish to be omniscient infects our understanding of human knowledge. It isn't a wish we can outgrow, since Kant thinks it is 'prescribed by the very nature of reason itself', but it's a wish that can be understood and contained. The longing to transcend human limits is as human as the fact that we cannot. At the heart of Kant's ethics, however, the wish is not only indulged but endorsed: we are to act only on those principles that we could will to be a universal law of nature. Kant's metaphysics remind us that we are not God; his ethics give us permission to pretend that we are. This is a method, and it isn't mad.[9]

This means that Emile has never experienced what Kant called the gap between *is* and *ought*. This is not just any old hardship, but the basic fact that *things go wrong*. You may want to protect your child from many things, but if you protect them from *that*, how on earth can they grow up? Though there's no evidence that Rousseau knew anything about Buddhism, Emile's environment is remarkably similar to the one Buddha's royal father tried to construct for his son, for whom he built three palaces to shield him from all knowledge of human suffering. At the age of twenty-nine, say the legends, Buddha ventured from the palace and saw decay, illness and death – shadows that fall on even the most fortunate of lives. The shock drove him towards a life of extreme asceticism, though after some years as a wandering beggar he found a more temperate path. Except for the palaces – Emile would prefer a country cottage – his metaphysical education is no different. Emile has not been prepared for any but the best of all possible worlds.

Now Rousseau thought most illnesses result from lack of proper diet and exercise. Even if modern medicine has confirmed that much sickness could be avoided by many of Rousseau's prescriptions – good air, physical activity, little meat, fresh fruit and vegetables – it does nothing to confirm his more important claim: that human beings are not naturally afraid of death. It's a claim he makes often, largely in order to undermine Hobbes, who thought fear of death so natural that it's reasonable to submit to the will of any old absolute sovereign who can stave off war for a while. We needn't go as far as Hobbes, nor believe in a terrifying afterlife, to find the thought of total annihilation appalling. The Austrian philosopher Jean Améry, who survived two years at Auschwitz, thought that even the most natural death is an affront to human reason more unbearable than any he experienced in the concentration camp. How can this whole world that is mine be slated for extinction? We learn, of course, to accept the fact of it, but it may be impossible to conceive it, however often we try. The fact that human beings begin potentially endless journeys that are arbitrarily cut short, that we are endowed with abilities to undertake projects – be they loves or works – that cannot be fulfilled in one lifetime, can seem the most monstrous cosmic joke. We may tell ourselves that mortality makes human lives richer, and it may even be true; next to Odysseus or Antigone, the Greek gods look flat. Still the Stoic air of indifference towards death often praised by Rousseau seems deeply inhuman. However you steel yourself, most deaths will produce, at least for a moment, the ache of response: *that* should not have happened. The throb in that moment is the pain of the gulf between *is* and *ought*. When it happens, even atheists may feel the pull of Christianity's understanding of death as punishment, though they may reject its promise of eternal life.

But forget about death, for the time being. Long before you have to face it, you will face other trials. Even the luckiest among us will stumble over pieces of the world that are not as they should be. How we react is the key to whether or not we grow up. In a perceptive passage of *Peter Pan*, Barrie describes what happens to the hero when Captain Hook returns his generous, chivalrous gesture with violence.

Not the pain of this but its unfairness was what dazed Peter. It made him quite helpless. Every child is affected thus the first time he is treated unfairly. All he thinks he has a right to when he comes to you to be yours is fairness. After you have been unfair to him he will love you again, but will never afterwards be quite the same boy. No one ever gets over the first unfairness; no one except Peter. He often met it, but he always forgot it. I suppose that was the real difference between him and all the rest. (*Peter Pan*, p. 113)

You have probably forgotten the details of your first unfairness, presumably because it happened very early, and was followed by many more. Still Barrie is probably right to say no one ever gets over it, and the reason Peter Pan remains an eternal child is that each succeeding unfairness is a surprise. None is ever internalized, so his trust in the world remains unscathed.

Not so for the rest of us; *Peter Pan* is a fairy tale. Even babies, as we'll see, sense and suffer from a world that doesn't fit. It's the beginning of alienation, but also of indignation that, if properly guided, will be needed to make a life active. What guidance is proper? We want our children to see as little suffering as possible, and we know that even Buddha's royal father couldn't shield him. Most of us have considerably fewer resources than he did. When my own son was eleven or twelve he came home from school complaining that a teacher had treated him unfairly, and hearing the details I thought he was right. Here's what I told him: *This won't be the last time that someone in power treats you unfairly. They may be threatened or jealous or simply tired, they may prefer the kid or the employee who flatters or falls. Besides reading and writing and arithmetic, one of the things you need to learn in school is how to live with that – without losing yourself.* Was the balance right? After too many encounters with unfairness I could not share his outrage. We want our children to remain awake to injustice; we just don't want them to be undone by it. I was rather pleased with my little speech; it was certainly better than anything I'd heard as a child, when my own parents' refusal to acknowledge that a teacher might be anything less than benign left me not only alone with my indignation but deeply confused: *weren't they just saying the* is *is the* ought? But the problem is one of proportion. The thought may be sustaining when the teacher in question is one among many; when such teachers are in the majority, you begin to suspect that your children would be better off out of school.

Even if confined to a single educator, it isn't a lesson Rousseau would have his pupil learn. Emile has been raised, you'll recall, in a world without masters and servants, authorities and subjects, precisely so he will not learn to tolerate injustice. It's possible that this could prepare him to resist it. But what if he finds it crippling, and can only react with the helpless daze of Peter Pan?

There are no empirical answers to this question; no one was raised like Emile. Let's give credit where it's due: even if his larger aim is to force them to become free adults, our attention to children's development began with Rousseau. He's been called the inventor of childhood itself.

> What must be thought of that barbarous education which sacrifices the present to an uncertain future, which burdens a child by making him miserable in order to prepare him for I know not what happiness he may enjoy? . . . Why do you want to fill with bitterness and pain those few years which go by so rapidly and can return no more for them than they can for you? (*Emile*, p. 79)

These are very good questions. But they do not let us avoid an even more pressing one: how do we prepare a child for a world that is not the way it should be?

2. Infancy, Childhood, Adolescence

Busy Being Born

What is so gripping about babies? They grip us in different degrees, of course, and even the most devoted of new parents may admit that babies are not *endlessly* fascinating; there is a certain amount of boredom involved in accompanying an infant through its very limited repertoire. Yet most of us are vulnerable to the tug of amazement that babies themselves express, and exert on us. What earlier ages attributed to Providence is likely to be chalked up to evolutionary advantage today. Given that they would die without adult attention, it's a good thing babies are born with the ability to capture it.

For the German Jewish philosopher Hannah Arendt, nothing about our fascination is contingent. In *The Human Condition* she argued that birth is a miracle:

> The miracle that saves the world, the realm of human affairs, from its normal, 'natural' ruin is ultimately the fact of natality, in which the faculty of action is

ultimately rooted. It is, in other words, the birth of new men and the new beginning, the action they are capable of by virtue of being born. (p. 247)

Arendt coined the term 'natality' – the fact that we are born – as a counterpoint to the familiar 'mortality', the fact that we die, which was so central to the ancient Greeks that their definition of human was simply 'mortal'. Traces of that centrality remain in the first syllogism most students of philosophy ever learn:

> All men are mortal
> Socrates was a man
> Therefore, Socrates was mortal

They also appear in the Greek-centred view of her teacher, the German philosopher Martin Heidegger, who held that consciousness of death is fundamental to being human. Against this tradition, Arendt's focus on birth is revolutionary; she held it to be the central category of political thought. (Much of her enthusiasm for the United States rested on the fact that it was a nation of immigrants: newly born into the state they could constantly renew it. It's a thought worth considering by European nations currently struggling with what they regard as the *problem* of immigration.) For Arendt, the origin of life from inorganic matter is so infinitely improbable that it prefigures every action:

The fact that man is capable of action means that the unexpected can be expected of him, that he is able to perform what is infinitely improbable. And this again is possible only because each man is unique, so that with each birth something uniquely new comes into the world. (*Human Condition*, p. 178)

For de Beauvoir, this newness is preserved beyond birth:

If, in all oppressed countries, a child's face is so moving, it is not that the child is more moving or that he has more of a right to happiness than the others; it is that he is the living affirmation of human transcendence: he is on the watch, he is an eager hand held out to the world, he is a hope, a project. (*The Ethics of Ambiguity*, p. 102)

Our gaze at the baby is thus not, or not only, a function of evolutionarily programmed survival strategies or plain parental silliness. Babies are miraculous. *Such tiny fingers (that will one day build or weave or shoot or caress), even tinier toes (that will dance or kick or swim or trudge). And all of it open.* Arendt's turn from mortality to natality shifts our focus. Cicero wrote that the task of philosophy is learning how to die; Arendt's emphasis on the improbable uniqueness of every human being, on the potential openness of each moment of our lives, makes growing up central, though she did not address it directly herself. 'Whenever we act, even in a small way, we are changing the course of history, nudging the world down one path rather than another,' writes psychologist Alison Gopnik in *The Philosophical Baby* (p. 23). This sentence was as true in Cicero's day as it is in ours, yet the consciousness of our capacity to change the world through our actions is one that the Enlightenment brought to the fore. For Arendt, that consciousness is what allows us to maintain faith and hope, features of experience the ancient Greeks – who counted hope as the last of the evils in Pandora's box – discounted, but that are celebrated in the glad tidings signalled by the birth of Jesus. For a non-Christian like Arendt, the miracle is not that particular birth. In the Christian celebration of the divine become human she sees a symbol of the wonder we glimpse every time a child is born: the miracle of a completely new being that might just redeem the world.

For the baby, the miracle is the world itself, in all its bits and pieces. Watch a baby investigate a set of keys or a crinkly bit of paper, and you will not only see an inseparable mixture of play and science but a touch of awe and wonder that would be called religious, if the baby had concepts to mark the sacred and profane. We envy that wonder, and we cannot get it back, for every experience of wonder contains an element of surprise. Gopnik suggests that when we travel we experience the world as babies do, the newness of our surroundings creating more vivid awareness and attention. Under very particular conditions this may be true in moments, but it cannot last for long. More than once I've had the good fortune to live in jaw-droppingly beautiful surroundings. My jaw did drop, the first few mornings, waking up overlooking Lake Como or Dingle Bay, till the surprise of it ceased and turned into pleasure, but the wonder was gone.

Once babies discover what we know – *it's just a set of keys with a function, produced rather often from pockets and handbags, not a mystery of jingling whatsits* – their own wonder fades. If they are lucky they'll go on to the next adventure, examining another bit of the world and moving from awe to understanding. The very fact that they can progress from viewing an object with awe to tasting it, turning it and taking it apart on occasion, should itself be a matter for wonder. For Kant, the fact that our cognitive capacities are fitted to comprehend something so utterly distinct from them – the rest of the world – was almost enough to make an argument for the existence of God. What else could ensure that the two fit together, allowing us to pick out laws of gravity or motion from the infinite amount of data that surrounds us? But since Kant put God's existence squarely outside the realm of knowledge, the baby's continued experience of the world yielding to her cognitive capacities produces not gratitude or humility, but an attitude some psychologists call confidence, and others simply trust. The baby who learns that pulling on a string makes the toy bird over her crib flap its wings has learned both to count on herself and the world to work in reliable ways, and together. In favourable circumstances, she will experience this so often that she has some reason to infer that the reliability of that relationship is infinite. Psychologists estimate that we learn more in the first three years of life than in all the rest of it. *That some things are wet and others sticky, some are hard enough to hurt and others soft enough to be shaped with our hands, that animals are not stones or vegetables, that night follows day and then back again, that children become adults but not trees or lions.* The discoveries we make are too many to remember, let alone count, and they do indeed hold up, these truths about the world. Why shouldn't they go on forever?

It makes little sense to speak of trust in the world where the practices of distrust are dormant, the possibilities of comparison nil. The baby has no choice but to go on in the world as if it were trustworthy. What other chance does she have? With good fortune in the form of a reasonably sane and responsive parent, the baby learns to trust. Along with basic categories of understanding like substance and causality, and laws of nature like gravity, the main thing babies learn is how other people work. *If you cry at the pain in your belly they will give you something warm and sweet that soothes it.* Rousseau was aware that infant feeding had an impact on adult development, which later psychologists corroborated while softening his views. Arguing against the practice of feeding infants according to schedule, the American psychoanalyst Haskell Bernstein wrote that the infant fed on schedule

> will have to endure the discomfort of hunger for longer periods of time, but equally important, for him there is no consistent correlation of hunger, crying, and being fed. The feeding, when it occurs, has no connection with his own activity – the restoration of equilibrium is arbitrary and the infant feels helpless to influence the course of events. (*Being Human*, p. 160)

Of course the baby has no concept of action or influence, any more than she has the concept of mother or self. It is through these processes that those concepts are formed, and much depends on the luck of the draw. Helpless as we are when thrown into the world, other people are crucial. The baby's hunger needs stilling as its exploration needs response. A depressed or abusive caregiver is unable to meet the baby's wonder. Where the baby seeks method, the inadequate caregiver sees nothing but mess. When we fail to marvel, for a moment, at the fact that the mush spills downward *every single time* it's splattered, we fail to respond to the buoyant aliveness that nearly every baby brings to the world – and we strangle it, just a little. Since we've long forgotten how we learned about gravity, and since we are the ones responsible for mopping the floor before someone slips on it, we will inevitably strangle, or choke off something. Still if we meet the baby's need for response often enough, we are part of the world that encourages her to develop trust in it.

Erik Erikson, the psychologist who argued that the baby's first task is to develop social trust, maintained that this trust cannot be complete. Erikson pointed to a trauma that the happiest of infants cannot avoid, and named teething as the point where good and evil enter her world. The baby's teeth begin to bore from within, from the same mouth that had been her main source of pleasure. Even worse, the pain caused by teething can only be assuaged by biting – which can only cause the mother to withdraw.

> This earliest catastrophe in the individual's relation to himself and to the world is probably the ontogenetic contribution to the biblical saga of paradise, where the first people on earth forfeited forever the right to pluck without effort what had been put at their disposal; they bit into the forbidden apple and made God angry. (*Childhood and Society*, p. 79)

Erikson argues that teething has prototypical significance, preparing us for a lifetime in which our most legitimate needs cannot be met by the world we are given. Like Peter Pan, we forget it, and under the right conditions we learn to suck without biting, to elicit the responses that will be crucial to developing basic trust in the world and our own ability to navigate it. 'But even under the most favorable circumstances, this stage leaves a residue of a primary sense of evil and doom and a universal nostalgia for a lost paradise' (Ibid, p. 80). Erikson concludes that it is against this sense of loss and division that basic trust must maintain itself, throughout our whole lives.

Watch a baby who has achieved it. Long before she has a language she can act on the world in myriad ways. *Smile, they smile back. Push, and it moves.* There are a thousand ways to get it wrong – I have seen babies coo in answer to the sound of wind in the trees – but with time, and adults who can mirror, fairly often, their own thrill at getting things right, babies learn what it means to act in and on the world. Every discovery is a triumph that affirms two things: the baby's own growing powers, and the transparency of the world. Off she goes, driven by the inborn propensity of human reason to seek what Kant called the Unconditioned.

Using Kant's imposing term to understand the normal development of curiosity may seem rather stretched, but the process he describes is as natural as it is straightforward. Reason involves the capacity to ask *why*, which itself presupposes a concept of possibility: *things could have been otherwise, why are they just like that?* The actual is given to us, without any conscious effort on our part; it takes reason to conceive the possible. Kant says reason was born when we left the Garden of Eden. Where everything is as it should be, what could induce us to imagine another state of affairs?

Contemporary psychologists believe the ability to imagine counterfactuals occurs early in the second year of life. Experiments show babies mentally anticipating the possibilities that a new tool will allow, rather than using trial and error strategies as chimpanzees do. What's clear is that not long after the child has learned language, her ability to imagine other states of affairs is enough to keep her asking, all day long, why something is this way rather than that. Once you start asking why, there's no natural place to stop. Why does it rain? Because the clouds are heavy and full of water. But that's not an answer until you know why water condenses and clouds become heavy. Perhaps you can give your child a clear account of rain and wind and thunder, but the better your explanations, the more likely your child is to ask for more. Even a meteorologist will reach a point where she must fall back on the rather helpless exclamation: *because that's the way the world is!* A child whose desire to explore has not been stifled will be inclined to reply: *why is the world that way?* The question need not be triggered by the weather; most anything will do. But once she starts asking for conditions – the grounds for something being the way it is, since she is now able to imagine its being otherwise – everything short of an explanation of the world as a whole is frustratingly partial. An explanation of the world as a whole must include an answer to why the world as a whole is just that way. And the only truly satisfying answer would be: because it's the best of all possible ones.

To reach this point would be to reach the Unconditioned – a point at which the world as a whole would make such perfect sense that no more questions can be asked at all. It is not a point in space/time, for it is never actually reachable. For Leibniz, its unattainability is contingent: if we could but live long enough to follow up every question, as God does, we would understand everything, as He does. That understanding must have a normative component, for if this world were not the best of all possible ones there would still be questions to ask (e.g., *Why not?*). For Kant, the fact that none of us is God – though we are continually tempted to long for the two most important divine attributes, omniscience and omnipotence – cannot be contingent; it's the most important fact about us. And whether or not we long for it, the best of all possible worlds is not a world we could live in and still be recognizably human.

Without a notion of the possible as well as the actual, babies cannot be said to believe they live in the best of all possible worlds, but they have no choice but to presume it. If Erikson is right, we lost this presumption when we gained our first tooth. Still the Unconditioned, if imaginable, would be remarkably like 'the harmless and safe condition of infant care, out of a garden, as it were, which cared for him without any effort on his part'.[10] It is no surprise that we yearn for this state of 'tranquil inactivity and constant peace'[11] – for much the same reason that we idealize early childhood. It may be more surprising that the first steps of reason, which are the steps of freedom away from infancy, should be focused on an imaginary object that would, if attained, bring us back to that immaturity and guardianship from which we have just emerged. Yet from the perspective of the small child as well as the dogmatic metaphysician, the process makes sense. If, as Kant says, the infancy of reason is dogmatic, it is characterized by children's unreflective self-confidence in their own powers, as well as the intelligibility of the world around them. The source of that self-confidence, he continues, is reason's initial success. The child experiences her increasing abilities together with the increasing coherence of the world around her with a growing sense that things make sense. *The world is my world: see how the two of us fit together!* A child, and perhaps a philosopher, who did not proceed down this path would be severely disturbed; calling Leibniz's metaphysics childish is not an insult. (Hegel was more tendentious in calling them a fairy tale.)

The idea of a world that ought to make sense is just what leads us to make what sense of it we can. The idea is so natural to human reason – and our partial successes in making sense so confirmed by experience – that we can hardly be blamed for expecting to reach it. Leibniz never actually thought mortals could get there, but he thought that a matter of time: nothing about the Unconditioned was for him in principle unreachable if our lives were only longer. It is the idea of a world that makes perfect sense which drives all our approximations to it: the understanding we seek when we engage in science and art as well as the transformations we seek when we pursue social justice. Could we ever achieve it, we'd have nothing more to seek at all; thus we'd be thrust back into a state resembling earliest infancy.

Kant offers these metaphors as consolation, for the Unconditioned is not an object but an idea that he likens to the horizon: it's a point you can move towards forever, but only children think it's a place you can actually reach. Dogmatism and trouble start when the Unconditioned is reified, that is, viewed as an object of absolute truth. The claim that there is no alternative but perdition to a worldview that shows how everything fits together and makes perfect sense is a mark of fundamentalism, whether of religious or market variety. In a child, such moments are appealing, necessary and usually harmless.

Don't Get Fooled Again

But you and the world only fit together so far. Young children create imaginary playmates and fantasy worlds; adults encourage them by filling books for young children with talking pigs or chickens, and books for older children with magic. Even very young children can distinguish such play from reality, however they may wish that the door to their own wardrobe might open to another world. This kind of mis-fit between yourself and the world is benign; better, it's creative. It's the result of the fact that we learn very early that more is possible than is actual, and it's the beginning of science and art. Experiments have shown that even those children whose imaginary companions are so vivid they may insist on their being fed or bathed alongside them know perfectly well that they're playing, and do so with relish.

There comes a moment, however, when you must recognize a gap; not merely between the world as it is and your own childish wishes (was it time travel? unicorns?) but between the world as it is and the world as it should be. You have witnessed some piece of injustice, however privileged you may be, or not. It can be as small as the playground bully or as big as all the suffering Buddha's royal father could not hide. Apparently even some animals perceive it. Primatologists Frans de Waal and Sarah Brosnan conducted a series of experiments in which pairs of Capuchin monkeys were rewarded for performing a small task with pieces of cucumber, food they normally enjoyed. Both willingly performed the task – returning a rock to the experimenters – until the experimenters rewarded one of the monkeys with a grape, food they enjoyed even more. At that, the monkey who got stuck with the cucumber revolted: throwing it back at the experimenter, refusing to participate any further. Interestingly enough, the monkeys restricted their outrage to the experimenter who was clearly the source of the injustice, not the other monkey who was the beneficiary of it. The experiment, repeated with different monkeys as well as other animals, suggests that a rough sense of fairness begins considerably further back on the phylogenetic tree than *Homo sapiens*. (Interesting as the experiment is to read about, it's astonishing to watch. Just google monkey+cucumber+grape to see an unforgettable expression of what is hard to call anything but moral outrage.) Parents of more than one child will find it very familiar.

Whether it's unequal reward for equal behaviour or outright violence, you have witnessed the gap between *is* and *ought*. One perfectly normal reaction – as the monkeys suggest – is rage. You may rage in all the wrong directions, but your indignation is perfectly justified. You have discovered what Nietzsche called the metaphysical wound at the heart of the universe.

Things are not as they should be, and you can neither get the *should* or the *things* out of your heart. One of the silliest suggestions in the history of philosophy is the idea that heart and head are necessarily divided, and one must trump the other. For David Hume, reason is 'impotent', and merely 'a slave to the passions'. Is it reason or passion that moves us? Most of us use both of them, in dialogue, most of the time, and never so much as when we witness unfairness. I'll return to Hume very shortly, after turning to Plato, whose *Republic* portrays a form of outrage so natural that it has repeated itself with somewhat tedious regularity for several millennia.

Not much is known about the ancient Greek Sophist Thrasymachus. Only a few fragments of his own writings survive. His name means 'fierce fighter', and Plato describes him entering a room like a wild beast about to spring. He has gone down in history as the anti-hero of the first great book of Western philosophy, who bursts into the house where Socrates and his friends are passing the time before dinner by talking about justice. In his sly old way, Socrates has asked his companions to define it, and proceeds to demolish all their definitions. Their attempts are shallow, conventional, in need of demolition: *telling the truth and giving back what you've borrowed? Helping your friends and hurting your enemies?* Socrates needs no more than a counterexample to dispense with each one.

Enter Thrasymachus. He is as young as he is wild, and his contribution to the discussion is, roughly: *bullshit*. Not his elders' definitions but the very fact that they are spending their time talking about justice and morality at all is what rouses his ire. Can they really be so naïve as to talk about morals? Don't they know that what we call morality is merely the invention of men holding power who construct a lot of rules to fool us into helping them maintain it? And what's wrong, by the way, with that? We are all of us out to serve our own interests, and it usually suits our interest to be immoral. No wonder the company has trouble defining justice: it's a fiction invented by strong men to keep weaker men down. Anyone who takes moral language seriously is not just a fool but a baby. In a striking piece of rhetoric Thrasymachus asks Socrates if perhaps he needs a nurse. It's the ultimate insult of a young man to his elder. For only a baby needing a nursemaid could fail to see the difference between sheep and shepherd: the sheep may believe the shepherd's care is devoted to the sheep's welfare, and it may continue to believe that all the way to the slaughterhouse.

Part of Thrasymachus' anger, and all of his insults, stem from his conviction of discovery. He is not, or not only, pleased to have seen through the deception his elders have swallowed. His rage is fuelled by disappointment. These are the men who ought to know better; they're his elders, after all. It is telling that the longest extant fragment of Thrasymachus' own writing speaks of the need for younger men to replace the old:

> I could wish, men of Athens, to have belonged to that long-past time when the young were content to remain silent unless events compelled them to speak, and while the older men were correctly supervising affairs of State. But since Fate has so far advanced us in time that we must obey others as rulers but must suffer the consequences ourselves . . . then it is necessary to speak.[12]

The regret in the words is rhetorical, but it also rings sincere. The youth's discovery leaves him ambivalent. There is no way to know how old Thrasymachus was when writing this fragment or conversing with Socrates, no way even to know if the encounter with Socrates was real. Yet in quite a different way than he intended, Plato captured a near-eternal truth in describing the adolescent indignation that the certainties he was raised on are shakier than they seemed, and the resolution to doubt absolutely everything thereafter. Kant could have been describing Thrasymachus in the following passage from the *Critique of Pure Reason*:

> He sees sophistical arguments, which have the attraction of novelty, set in opposition to sophistical arguments which no longer have that attraction, but

on the contrary tend to arouse the suspicion that advantage has been taken of his youthful credulity. And accordingly he comes to believe that there can be no better way of showing that he has outgrown childish discipline than by casting aside those well-meant warnings; and accustomed as he is to dogmatism, he drinks deep draughts of the poison, which destroys his principles by a counter-dogmatism. (A755/B783)

The other interlocutors in Plato's dialogues are little more than foils for Socrates. Unlike them, Thrasymachus makes Socrates feel fear. And no wonder: the problem with Thrasymachus' critique is not that it's false. He has put his finger on some of the lies on which conventional authority depends. If you cannot think of a statesman who has trumpeted a moral principle that he does not practise, with which he hopes to lull his public into silence, you haven't been paying attention to the news. Having seen through several such instances, Thrasymachus is determined to reject everything that smacks of moral principle at all. What was advertised as just policy turned out to be self-aggrandizement; Thrasymachus henceforth will deny that anyone can act justly for any reason other than self-aggrandizement. Let us call him the first post-modern nihilist. He's the first to offer the argument that claims of morality are the product of somebody seeking power trying to deceive us combined with a portion of self-deception – an argument that has re-appeared, with varying degrees of sophistication, from Machiavelli to Hobbes to Foucault. One thing common to all these thinkers – as well as to your neighbour or teenager – is a sense of revelation. This sense can't be simply the product of the familiar desire to say something new. Embarrassed by his earlier readiness to believe his pious, dogmatic elders, Thrasymachus is resolved: he won't be fooled again. For he is convinced that he's seen through everything. It takes a grown-up to know that this doesn't mean he's seen it.

If Thrasymachus was the first recorded thinker to suggest that morality is nothing but self-interested, deceptive rhetoric, Plato was the first to think the right response was to provide morality with foundations. It cannot work, as Hume would so elegantly show: you cannot derive an *ought* from an *is*. Plato's attempt to answer Thrasymachus by providing a metaphysics to undergird the reality of morals produced great philosophy – all ten books of *The Republic* – but not even Plato's student Aristotle thought it worked. No wonder every age produces a crop of Thrasymachuses, each one defiantly unmasking ideas of virtue as the triumph of a stronger faction that has managed to trick a weaker one into believing it. And each act of unmasking is presented as tough, and radically truthful: you may be fooled by all that noble-sounding rhetoric, but I'm bold and honest enough to see through the manipulations behind it.

Those who forget that this sort of argument goes back to Plato's day usually imagine that earlier ages were as naïve as they were golden. (Or gilt, as it were.) Religion, they believe, was the rock on which morality was grounded, and the truths which people based their lives on were secure and unquestioned; only now can we see through the apparent religious and moral certainties to their true, manipulative basis. Just a little history – or a glance at bloody contemporary battles between Sunni and Shiite Muslims, for example – should give the lie to the suggestion that religiously dominated societies are more secure than we are. God may have reigned in His heaven (though atheists doubted His existence fairly early on), but His nature was the subject of debates more complex and passionate than any we have today. Armies of men slaughtered one another regularly to prove one conception or another, and Socrates was put to death for offending religion in the birthplace of Western thought. Small wonder that sceptical challenges to *all* established doctrines are almost as old as those doctrines themselves. If you've witnessed much of this sort of unmasking, you may agree with the English philosopher Bernard Williams that it soon becomes immensely boring, and explains very little: claims that knowledge is reducible to power cannot even 'explain the difference between listening to someone and being hit by them'.[13]

For Kant, however, the movement from dogmatic certainty to radical scepticism was crucial to the process of growing up:

> The first step in matters of pure reason, marking its infancy, is *dogmatic*. The second step is *skeptical* and indicates that experience has rendered our judgment wiser and more circumspect . . . Skepticism is thus a resting-place for human reason, where it can reflect upon its dogmatic wanderings and make survey of the region in which it finds itself, so that for the future it may be able to choose its path with more certainty. (A761/B789)

Unsurprisingly, Kant holds that while scepticism may be a necessary resting-place, it is not a permanent dwelling. Still he is adamant in opposing every attempt to censor sceptical positions, for 'The skeptic is the taskmaster who constrains the dogmatic reasoner to develop a sound critique of the understanding and reason' (A769/B797).

Kant is surely speaking autobiographically; if it was Rousseau who changed his life and gave it direction, it was Hume, he wrote, who awoke him from dogmatic slumber. Both men presented sceptical objections to long-entrenched views. Earlier we saw how Rousseau's rage at the established order not only produced a critique more detailed and incisive than that of Thrasymachus; it also left room for action that was something other than Thrasymachus' cynical acquiescence to whatever power happens to rule. This kind of scepticism is harmless, for its unmasking is potentially endless. If *every* moral claim is a mask for a claim to power, why not help yourself to a portion of whiskey or weed or similar anaesthetic, and settle in with the powers that be? The impulse to demystify may have to precede the will to change, but it is far from being all that is needed for it. Rousseau's critique of the power relations masked by ideology is certainly as trenchant as that of Thrasymachus, whose rhetorical skills never sufficed to produce images like the garlands woven by artists and intellectuals to mask the chains that bind us all. Yet both proceed from that indignation, so natural in adolescents, at the disjunct between the way the world is, and the way, something tells them, it ought to be.

That indignation may be directed at the false promise of natality itself. Every birth may hold the promise of a completely new beginning, but every experience reveals, soon enough, that we are born into webs of relations that constrain as they sustain us. As soon as we're old enough to have gathered much experience, we must acknowledge that the world into which we were born is already given, and rarely yields to our will. Much of the time we do not even fit together with it. In offering programmes for radically restructuring the given world, Rousseau took one path that many adolescents forge. Incensed by the discovery that the world is not what it should be, many a youth has taken up the sort of idealism for which youth is known, and often dismissed. (The expression 'Anyone who isn't a socialist at twenty has no heart, anyone who is still a socialist at forty has no head' is an expression of several misconceptions, not least about the relations between heart and head, but it is also an expression of contempt.) To be sure, the youthful outrage at the gap between *is* and *ought* can be exhausting. This kind of sceptic is always posing questions we cannot answer, and rarely stays long enough to listen to our attempts at reply. Is life really long enough to be subjected to this sort of thing – over and over and over? 'I never want to see that man again,' said Denis Diderot of his erstwhile good friend Rousseau. 'He makes me believe in devils and hell.' It's not hard to understand how a constant, lifelong battle to undo the *is* could drive the man crazy, and most of the people around him as well. And we have seen how Rousseau's insistence on creating a world that makes sense ultimately vitiates his attempt to educate a child for a world that does not. It is nevertheless a more fruitful consequence of indignation than the sputtering put-downs of Thrasymachus. Instead of resting with critique in the space between *is* and *ought*, Rousseau proposes a way forward; it's up to us to decide how far we want to go.

Whether accompanied by the sort of idealism Rousseau embodied, or the disdain we saw in Thrasymachus, rage is not the only reaction to the gap between *is* and *ought*. More common in our time is the sort of urbane knowingness so present in David Hume. Born in 1711 in comfortable circumstances in Scotland, the man who would become the most important philosopher in the English language never succeeded in obtaining an academic position, nor in gaining the recognition as the Newton of the mind for which he longed. After what he called 'a very feeble trial' at business as the clerk for a Bristol sugar merchant, he was chiefly employed in a series of diplomatic posts that took him to Vienna, Turin and, most significantly, Paris, where he met the major figures of the Enlightenment salons. One of these was Rousseau, who was in danger of arrest for *Emile*'s attack on established religion. Sympathetic to the latter (one wonders what he would have made of the rest of the book), Hume arranged refuge in England for the Swiss fugitive, but dislike of conventional religion was the only thing the two men had in common, and the relationship soon soured. Accounts of their falling-out usually blame Rousseau, who accused Hume of fomenting a conspiracy against him, but whatever the immediate cause of their quarrel, it is hard to imagine two more different souls. Where Rousseau was suspicious of irony, Hume was suspicious of earnestness; where Rousseau took the gap between *is* and *ought* to demand a reshaping of the world, Hume preferred to give up the *ought*. Had he not written that any text that concerned neither mathematical reasoning nor matters of fact should be committed to the flames, 'for it can contain nothing but sophistry and illusion'?[14] Mathematics and matters of fact: the *ought* was clearly neither. In a famous passage of his *Treatise of Human Nature* (1739) Hume formulated the problem more clearly than anyone before him:

> In every system of morality, which I have hitherto met with, I have always remarked, that the author proceeds for some time in the ordinary way of reasoning . . . when of a sudden I am surprised to find, that instead of the usual copulation of propositions, *is* and *is not*, I meet with no proposition that is not connected with an *ought* or *ought not*. This change is imperceptible but is, however, of the last consequence. For . . . this *ought* or *ought not* expresses some new relation or affirmation.[15]

The *ought* is no part of the world, and cannot be inferred from anything in it. You can find out the fact that 8 million children in the world are working as slave labourers, on best current estimates, but nothing about the fact itself can tell you that it ought not to be so. The fact describes the way the world is; to get to the judgement that it ought to be different you need to make a leap. For Hume, the leap could not be made with reason, which he considered impotent; he held every such judgement to be a matter of passion. If the contemplation of child labour makes you feel bad, you will condemn it; if it does not, you will yawn. Reason, in any case, has nothing to say about the matter at all.

I find the coolness with which Hume surveys the split between ourselves and the world to be chilling, though I can't but acknowledge his achievement. He writes as if he were merely pointing out a small matter of logic his predecessors had overlooked, but his argument goes straight to the heart of most questions ever raised about the human condition. We cannot derive what we should do in the world from any fact about it. So why not just leave it to humankind to make it up as we go along? The making up isn't arbitrary; Hume thought that general psychological mechanisms explain why some habits and customs take hold and others do not. But mechanisms, however general, are not reasons, nor can they even be causes, on Hume's account of the latter. They are just the way things are.

Expressed in the calmest of terms, Hume's critique is far more devastating than Thrasymachus'. For Thrasymachus, morality was *in fact* all made up to mask existing power relations. This is, he rants, the way of the world, but he offers no reasons for believing it must be that way. Hume is far deeper, for he means to leave us without a conceptual leg to stand on. It's a matter of logical structure: what is, just *is*, and any claim about what *ought* to be is a claim about our own wishes and desires. Why ever should we imagine that the two would be related? Children, even as metaphors, being largely absent from his writing, Hume never actually describes the desire to connect *is* and *ought* as childish, but the placidly withering tone in which he writes suggests that anyone who baulks at his conclusions is hopelessly naïve.

For Hume's intentions are anything but revolutionary. His sceptical reflections have so little consequence that he doesn't even take them seriously enough to let his life be disturbed by them. Within his study, he can prove that we have no real knowledge of any of the propositions our lives are based on: that the sun will rise tomorrow morning, that killing your father is an unspeakable crime, even that any one event ever caused another.

> Where am I, or what? From what causes do I derive my existence, and to what condition shall I return? . . . I am confounded with all these questions, and begin to fancy myself in the most deplorable condition imaginable, environed with the deepest darkness, and utterly deprived of the use of every member and faculty.[16]

Fortunately, he continues, all it takes is a good meal, a game of backgammon and a couple of merry friends to dispel 'this philosophical melancholy and delirium', which is bound to look ridiculous after a few glasses of sherry. Lest this all reek too strongly of the unflappability of a British clubhouse, it must be remembered that Hume's doubts on one subject did have real personal consequences. Rumours of his atheism prevented him from attaining a university position, and his most brilliant book, the *Dialogues Concerning Natural Religion* (1779), could only be published posthumously. On every other matter, however, Hume was prepared not only to defer to custom and habit, but to make them the foundation of our lives. It is custom and habit that lead us to believe the sun will rise tomorrow morning, and that when it does we will continue to shoot billiards in the belief that a perfect shot at the red will cause the others to roll in our favour. Custom and habit, without considerable reflection, have always been the grounds for what we do, for observation tells us too little, and reason is too weak a guide. We've no better option than to let custom and habit carry us on.

Reliance on custom and habit is reasonable enough if we're contemplating the planet's turning, or even ordinary moral questions. The consequences of Hume's views become problematic, however, when applied to the political world. You may find the fact that children are forced to labour in mines or kitchens or brothels to be appalling. But since justice is not a matter of fact or mathematics, the fact that you are appalled is just that: a fact about you and your emotions – what sorts of things you happen to loathe or like. In Hume's day, it happened to be a matter of custom and habit that thousands of children in the cities where he lived passed their lives in service hardly better than slavery. It was indeed such a matter of custom and habit that hardly a man of letters thought it worth comment. David Hume certainly didn't. It would take more than a century and a powerful labour movement, fuelled by ideas of justice that cannot arise from experience (that did not yet contain them), to bring about the end of child labour in Britain. Meanwhile, Hume's primary passion, 'love of literary fame', was finally satisfied when his six-volume *History of England* became a bestseller. None of his philosophical treatises received much notice in his lifetime, and the British Library still lists him as 'David Hume, historian'.

The *History* was less popular in the New World. Thomas Jefferson had it banned from the University of Virginia for fear it 'will spread universal Toryism across the land'. Samuel Johnson demurred, arguing that Hume wasn't really a Tory, for he 'has no principle; if anything he is a Hobbist'. This is not the place to trace the Tory relation to Hobbes, but Hume was considered the father of modern British Conservatism, and Edmund Burke's attack on the French

Revolution drew heavily on Hume's views. What is certain is that Hume's metaphysics leave no room for reflective challenge to established orders. The space between *is* and *ought* is the space where questions arise. If you drop the *ought* as unfounded, where are you to begin?

Hume's voice can sound like the voice of a grown-up, with strong echoes of *Peter Pan*'s Mr Darling. British philosopher Isaiah Berlin praised it as 'calm, reasonable, placid, moderate, ironical, with a firm sense of reality, and lucid and disciplined prose'.[17] In praising Hume as opposed to the anti-rationalists, Berlin suggests that the absence of passion is enough to make something rational. Hume's tone can be soothing, unfailingly calm, comfortably obliging. *Have another glass of sherry and your doubts will disappear.* The French didn't call him 'Le Bon David' for nothing. The sun will go up and then down as it ever has, with or without ideas of causation or justice or law. It's a voice of the sort of resignation that is meant to comfort, and many a reader has been comforted. If ideas and ideals are chimerical, there's no point in deploring the gap between *ought* and *is*, much less in doing anything to reduce it. Your desire for a standpoint that makes your condemnation of slave labour something weightier than your distaste for codfish is a relic of childish wishes, your desire to be part of a better world of a piece with your earlier fantasies of opening a door into Narnia.

If such sentiments sound grown-up, it's because we've been fooled by a false idea of maturity. Rousseau and Hume represent two reactions to the discovery of the mismatch between *is* and *ought*. While it's too simple to say that Rousseau disdained the former as Hume disdained the latter, neither was inclined to give each his due. It would take Kant to appreciate the fact that we must take both seriously – if we are ever to arrive at an adulthood we need not merely acquiesce in but can actively claim as our own.

Dissatisfied Minds

By the time you are old enough to pick up a book like this one, you have already learned it: the world is not your world, and you don't have another. The wonder you felt as a very small child may be echoed in moments; a great work of music, a glorious landscape, a new love story, giving birth yourself can all bring it on. (If it turns out to be the latter you'll be forced to remind yourself that not all of the infant's encounters with the world produce wonder. There's a great deal of fear and frustration as well. It's consolation, of a sort.) But those moments are echoes, and few. They can provide occasion for gratitude but also for melancholy, insofar as they recall, however dimly, a time when they were so many they seemed to fill the world. Once all it took to produce awe and wonder was a bunch of keys; now you have to travel to Yosemite, or the west coast of Ireland. Some claim that the right sort of mindfulness training can lead you to find it in a leaf or a cup of coffee. I never got the hang of it, though that may be a personal failing, but even those who claim to achieve a sense of wonder at the ordinary acknowledge that it takes a lot of work.

You've accepted the dimming of sparkle. (What looked opalescent was just dew on the grass.) Further: your shock at the fact that the world is not only less sparkly, but downright hideous in places, has begun to wear off. Some bits of injustice still pull you up short – the long prison sentence for a hapless whistleblower, say, when men who ordered torture remain not just at large but in demand. Perhaps it's something as simple and immediate as the promotion your flashy co-worker got at the office while your quieter efforts went unacknowledged. However wrenching any such experiences can be, they no longer have you feeling on the edge of abyss, watching the void between *is* and *ought* open before your eyes. You have seen it before, which means you've begun to get used to it. Some of us get cucumbers while others get grapes, and most days your indignation is as hard to access as the wonder that preceded it.

This can sound like growing up, which is one reason so many people are afraid of it. With the passing of time and the accumulation of experience, things get repeated, and the more the repetition the less the surprise. As surprise recedes, so does passion. The facts are the same, but you no longer feel them as acutely. And isn't that a boon? Life is dimmer and duller, but it doesn't hurt so much, either. Those of us who once thrilled to dance and dream until dawn are now content to retire rather earlier to a good bed and pillow. The edge is missing, but so is the hangover. You have learned not to count much on the things outside you: friends and fortune can disappear, and you've seen lives upended by floods, famine or war. The solution, you conclude, can only be found inside you. You cannot control much else, but with determination and practice you can learn to control your own emotions, at least enough to ensure that what goes on outside affects you less. You've already accepted the gap between you and the world in principle; what remains is the task of embracing it in practice. The world is unstable, sometimes treacherous, and immeasurably vast; your soul, by contrast, is sufficiently limited and malleable to be the sort of thing you might transform. You will sleep better, and hurt less, if you turn your sights inward, for a good soul is in reach when nothing else is.

The pot-bellied uncle who offers this sort of advice has been reading the Stoics, or the bastardized bits of them that can be found in many a modern self-help manual, but he hasn't studied Kant. To be fair, Kant's worldview is easily confused with a Stoic one. Like every educated man of his day he grew up reading the

Roman philosophers, and some of their tropes can be found in his work. The beginning of his *Foundation of the Metaphysics of Morals* (1785) could pass for an excerpt from Cicero or Marcus Aurelius, and was presumably influenced by them. Kant begins his best-known work of ethics with a quick reminder that gifts of fortune – power and riches, health and happiness – are worth nothing at all without virtue. The only good, therefore, which is good in itself, is a good will.

> Even if it should happen that, owing to special dis-favour of fortune, or the niggardly provision of a step-motherly nature, this will should wholly lack power to accomplish its purpose, if with its greatest efforts it should yet achieve nothing, and there should remain only the good will (not, to be sure, a mere wish, but the summoning of all means in our power), then, like a jewel, it would still shine by its own light, as a thing which has its whole value in itself. (*Metaphysics of Morals*, p. 1)

This may sound like the sort of thing you could find in Boethius, whose *Consolation of Philosophy* was the most widely copied work of European secular literature throughout the early modern period. Its translators included King Alfred, Elizabeth I and Chaucer. Written in 524 while its author was in prison awaiting a particularly horrible form of execution, the book takes the form of a dialogue between Boethius and a vision of wisdom he calls Lady Philosophy. Poor Boethius laments that he did nothing but follow Plato's maxim that states would be better if ruled by philosophers. Now his turn from private study to public life has been rewarded with an accusation of treason. What solace, then, can philosophy offer? Lady Philosophy responds with disquisitions on the jewel-like nature of virtue, outshining any of fortune's gifts, but she goes considerably further: ill fortune, she claims, is positively preferable.

> For when good Fortune seems to fawn on us, she invariably deceives us with the appearance of happiness, adverse Fortune is always truthful, and shows by her mutability that she is inconstant. The first deceives, the second instructs; the first, with her manifestation of deceitful blessings, shackles the minds of those who enjoy them, whereas the second frees them through making them realize the frailty of happiness.[18]

Nor does she shirk from specifics. With her aid, says Lady Philosophy, 'Socrates won the victory of an unjust death.'

If you are facing execution, any form of bad faith that serves to console you is probably forgivable. And in a time when only half of children born survived to adulthood, it's easier to make allowances for the frequent Stoic suggestion that you should remind yourself that your children could be dead tomorrow whenever you kiss them. Calling Socrates' death fortunate, and your child's death probable, is meant to steel you against such events by reducing the pain and rage they produce. Can the events themselves harm you, if you train your emotions properly? For 'Outward things cannot touch the soul, not in the least degree . . . Get rid of the judgement, get rid of the "I am hurt", you are rid of the hurt itself' (Marcus Aurelius, *Meditations*, v.19; viii.40).

Just try it sometime. Even for small hurts like sprained ankles it is hard to pull off, though I recently found myself sprawled on a Berlin sidewalk repeating 'It's just pain, it will pass'. But even this, of course, was not an attempt to deny the hurt, as Marcus Aurelius suggested, just to remind myself that it was finite. For real pain – the loss of a love or a life – such mantras will be futile. Kant thought the Stoic advice was made for gods, not for humans, though gods, presumably, get on perfectly well without it. The Stoics imagine we can remedy our dissatisfaction with the world by working on the dissatisfaction. By whittling down our passions to the point where nothing in the world can provoke them, we can gain both independence and contentment. A mind satisfied in the consciousness of its own virtue is, for the Stoics, not only the highest but the only true good, for nothing can destroy it.

Contrary to many a rumour, Kant had nothing against passion. He explicitly denies that passions are the source of evil, and believes we should work on cultivating the right ones. Like anyone else with a shred of common sense, Kant knew that the happier people are when they do what they ought to, the likelier they are to do it. And like any good Enlightenment pedagogue, Kant sought ways to do so without false advertising – like promising that doing what you ought to do will automatically make you happy. Earlier philosophers operated with a sleight of hand, identifying happiness and virtue through one foul compromise or another. Epicureans insisted that happiness is virtue: following your (enlightened) self-interest creates more than harm. If this view, for Kant, is self-serving and lazy, that of the nobler-seeming Stoics is positively deluded. You can tell yourself that all the goods of the world are but vanity, that true happiness consists in virtue, and if it helps you hold your head high while facing execution then not much can be said against it. You are nonetheless denying a basic truth of existence: virtue is one thing, and happiness another, and though they may meet on many an occasion they are as fundamentally separate as you and the world. It's this truth that honesty and maturity demand you accept.

Nietzsche called Stoicism a slave morality, consolation designed for the powerless by the powerless. It's a nasty dig at Epictetus, who was in fact born in slavery, though other major Stoics included emperors like Marcus Aurelius, whose observation of the fickleness of fortune led him to focus on the one thing he thought we can control: the content of our souls. For Kant this means the Stoic is doubly guilty of bad faith. While he called himself a transcendental psychologist, he was also a remarkable ordinary one. Kant's awareness of our inclinations to self-deception is clear and profound. We never can be certain of what goes on in our souls, and though more recent developments like psychoanalysis can uncover pieces of self-deception, not even Freud thought we could get rid of it altogether. If we're honest, we know we're liable to exalt our better tendencies and to deny our baser ones – not only to others but first and foremost to ourselves. We may try to live honourably, but we can never know if we're successful, and the more certain we feel of our virtue, the less likely we are to possess it. The Stoic's attempt to control *something* by controlling his soul is thus ultimately impossible, and likely to lead to smugness or self-righteousness to boot.

Double bad faith: for the claim that virtue is all there is to happiness is an eloquent variation on the fox's sour grapes. Had he been able to secure happiness, he would savour its sweetness. Human desire for happiness is not something trivial. Nor is it a matter of passions that might be cooled or fanned. The key to Kant's view can be found in the very opening of the *Metaphysics of Morals*, which seems to echo the Stoics. Good will shines like a jewel, all right, but it is also the indispensable condition of being worthy of happiness. By introducing the notion of *being worthy of happiness* Kant introduces a notion of reason. If you have lived – as much as you can try, as far as you can tell – so as to be worthy of happiness and consistently fail to obtain it, not your passion but your reason will rebel.

It is reason that leads you to hold that the world should make sense. Not that it *does*; that's the error of children, Leibniz, Hegel and other dogmatic thinkers. Reason is the source of what Kant called regulative principles, ideas that do not tell us what the world is like but that orient our actions within it. Reason drives your search to make sense of the world by pushing you to ask why things are as they are. For theoretical reason, the outcome of that search becomes science; for practical reason, the outcome is a more just world. A world in which those who are worthy of happiness are subject to misery and oppression is a world out of joint, and reason must find that intolerable. Go ahead, try to think it: *children should be tortured, and those who torment them should be rewarded with fortune and fame.* The Marquis de Sade asserted it, but his own transgressions never approached those of his fictional characters, and one suspects that even he couldn't really maintain the claim. We know, of course, that we live in a world where the righteous suffer as often as the wicked flourish, but to think that it *ought to be that way* is beyond our ken. The mind reels.

But wait, you may ask. *Didn't Hume teach us that the* ought – *unlike the* is – *cannot be found in experience?*

Indeed he did. That's part of what awoke Kant from dogmatic slumber. What Kant called the Copernican turn in philosophy, his entire metaphysics, was spurred by Hume's scepticism, which led him to map the components of experience. 'The celebrated David Hume was one of those geographers of human reason who have imagined that they have sufficiently disposed of all such questions by setting them outside the horizon of human reason – a horizon which yet he was not able to determine' (*Critique of Pure Reason*, A760/B788). Kant's own geography would make different use of the horizon, as a point to which reason's efforts are all directed and, like any horizon, can never reach. A traveller in a desert or a sailor on the sea may go a very long way by keeping it in sight; similarly, reason's attempt to find the Unconditioned cannot be successful, but reason will be spurred ever further by fixing on it. First, however, reason must survey its own powers, the task of the *Critique of Pure Reason*.

This book cannot attempt to do justice to that one. For our present purposes it's enough to say that the *Critique* proved Hume's conception of experience to be so austere that it could not resemble human experience at all. Scepticism is not a new phenomenon, a fact Kant noted in calling it a natural part of reason's coming of age. Pointing out reason's weakness and folly is a sport that goes back to the early Greek

Sophists, at the very least. What made Hume's scepticism more powerful than theirs was not only the rhetorical brilliance of his exposition. Even more important was his reliance on the model of Newtonian physics, which had set a new standard for intellectual achievement. Newton seemed to present a model of knowledge that was absolutely certain, in contrast to all that had gone before it; henceforth there was the hard data of science, and everything else. The young Hume thought the latter should be committed to the flames, for if it contained anything but mathematical formulae and the direct observation of experience, it contained nothing but illusion. And this includes not only dogmatic metaphysics, but most of the assumptions on which we base our lives.

Kant's strategy was to argue that Hume's account of experience was too limited to account for it at all. If our minds worked as Hume said they do, Newtonian science, as well as far more pedestrian sorts of intellectual activity, would be impossible. On Kant's model, we are both more and less a part of the world than Hume thought. Data do not come to us without mediation, but are shaped and moulded by categories our minds contribute to make up experience. To view this as a *problem* is to imagine the sort of unmediated experience that is presumably only possible for God. Hume was right to point out that we don't perceive causes the way we perceive balls and billiard cues, for *cause* is a concept that we bring to the world. Far from making our experience of one thing's causing another a subjective habit, Kant's Transcendental Deduction showed that causality is a necessary condition of having any coherent experience at all. Without it, and other categories like substance and unity, we wouldn't perceive objects, much less relations between them. Perhaps we would experience a chaotic barrage of sensory data, but we can't even be certain of that.

Kant's map of our minds divides them into faculties, which we may think of as functions, and it's important to keep them straight. If the forms of space and time through which we perceive any data are provided by what Kant called sensibility, and if the concepts that allow us to perceive objects are provided by the understanding, what is the role of reason, which he called the highest faculty? Reason, we saw earlier, is what allows us to ask why. It is through sensibility and understanding that the world as it is – the totality of nature – is experienced. Through its idea of the Unconditioned – a world that makes sense as a whole – reason takes a step back.

It's the step back that allows us to ask questions and make judgements about experience. Unlike the forms provided by sensibility and understanding, reason isn't a necessary part of experience. Experience is conceivable without it, but just barely. Very young babies, caught up in the business of taking in the world they are given, may do without it. As soon as they begin to imagine that a state of affairs could be otherwise, and wonder why it isn't, they are using the same reason that will allow them to wonder why apples fall, how the moon and the tides are connected, and whether there might be general laws that explain them. Without the faculty of reason that Hume so disparaged, his revered Newton would be stuck in the orchard, gazing up at a tree.

Kant's answer to Hume is at the same time his reply to the Stoics. For the very same reason that is necessary for science is also the source of moral law. A world that makes sense – the overriding idea of reason – must make sense as a whole. The same drive that allows us to imagine that things could be different than they are given to us functions in science and social justice alike. It isn't a matter of likes or dislikes, a wish or a passion, but a need of our reason that cannot be extirpated. It can be denied, in rage or resignation, but never entirely destroyed. For the Stoic, the refusal to accept the world as it's given is a matter of human weakness that may be cured by changing your emotions. For Kant that refusal is precisely human strength. Later writers held that our inability to accept reality stems from infantile wishes that we ought to grow out of. For Kant it stems from the voice of critical reason, and it's a voice that needs to be heard.

On this account, philosophy itself is a crucial part of growing up. Unsurprisingly enough, many philosophers tend to think so, but they think so in very different ways. Hegel, for example, thought that 'the aim of philosophy is to defend reality against its detractors' (*Introduction to the Lectures on World History*, p. 67). In showing us that reality is reasonable, Hegel aimed to make us content. Heine called him the German Pangloss, and in fact the mighty professor acknowledged his debt to Leibniz:

> Our investigation can be seen as a theodicy, a justification of the ways of God (such as Leibniz attempted in his own metaphysical manner, but using categories that were as yet abstract and indeterminate). It should enable us to comprehend all the ills of the world, including the existence of evil, so that the thinking spirit may yet be reconciled with the negative aspects of existence. (Ibid, p. 43)

Arguing that the real is rational, against appearances that suggest the opposite, has always been a daunting task involving extremely complicated intellectual exercise. Leibniz thought only God was in a position to carry it out. There is considerable indication that Hegel identified with God, which may have tempted him to try demonstrating what Leibniz merely asserted. Suppose someone showed you that what Hegel himself called the slaughterbank of history was part of a necessary and inevitable plan for moving humankind forward, and your indignation at the slaughter was just as short-sighted as the infant's distress when she cuts her first teeth. As the baby might be consoled could she know that teething is part of a process that makes her distinctively human, so you should be reassured that the appearances of unfairness that provoke your outrage are an absolutely necessary part of history's plan. Philosophy as lullaby? Hegel, like Leibniz, has the curious effect of bringing us back to the place where we accept the given as given, not because we have followed the Stoic's advice to detach ourselves from it, but because we have understood something about the nature and necessity of the given itself.

For Kant, by contrast, philosophy's role in helping us grow up is precisely the opposite. It will not console or soothe you; it is practically guaranteed to make your life harder. For the real is *not* rational, and reason's task is to make sure we never forget it. In leading us through the dialectic between dogmatism and scepticism, philosophy leads us to honour the wonder and the indignation that are present in both. It demands that we learn the difference between *is* and *ought* without ever giving up on either one. Hegel thought this process results in an unhappy consciousness, and the young Nietzsche called Kant's philosophy tragic. Neither of them is entirely wrong. Keeping one eye on the way the world ought to be, while never losing sight of the way it is, requires permanent, precarious balance. It requires facing squarely the fact that you will never get the world you want, while refusing to talk yourself out of wanting it.

This is what Kant meant when he wrote that growing up is less a matter of knowledge than of courage. The gulf between *is* and *ought* can turn into an abyss, sometimes, all the more if you understand that it isn't an accidental occurrence but a feature of most of the experiences you will ever have. Many people around you are inclined to deny this. These days, most of them do so not by trying to convince you that the world is reasonable – the evidence against *that* claim is overwhelming, and growing daily – but by denying the force of the *ought*. 'It is what it is' has become a common American expression, said with a touch of Stoic sigh to comment on some state of affairs that looks particularly hopeless. Insisting that it ought to be different will often earn you the kind of bemused condescension reserved for the child who kicks the chair that caused her to stumble.

It takes courage to insist that a regime that may kill, torture or jail you ought to be different, and we rightly honour those who are able to find it. That kind of courage is never easy, but it is usually straightforward. It is often easier to muster than the courage to withstand the various forms of ridicule with which more democratic cultures undermine their critics. It's an embarrassing fact that we are often more afraid of embarrassment than a host of other discomforts, but it isn't less true for all that. How often have you refrained from voicing hope or indignation for fear of being dismissed as childish? Oddly enough, *that* fear is adolescent, born of a time when few things feel worse than being regarded as less grown-up than your peers. Here Kant can help, not by providing consolation, but by assuring you that your failure to be consoled by one or another version of Stoicism is not *your* failure. You are right to be outraged. A satisfied mind is no substitute for a world in which behaviour is appropriately rewarded – by a grape instead of a cucumber, if that's the going rate. Where the balance between behaviour and reward is out of kilter it needs to be repaired, not by working on your own demands for reparation but by working on the world.

If the idea of a right to happiness is not an idle piece of wishful thinking but a demand of reason, the consequences can be revolutionary. This is part of what German philosopher Walter Benjamin meant in calling post-Kantian attempts like Hegel's to unify reason and nature, *ought* and *is*, 'eleventh-hour reactionary flights from the *honesty* of Kant's dualism'.[19] This kind of honesty takes courage, because the impossibility of bringing reason and nature together is not a truth we really want to know.

3. Becoming Adult

Education

If growing up is a matter of holding the *is* and the *ought* in balance, it will never be a stable position: each will always seek the upper hand. Hence growing up is not a task that ever stops. (Perhaps *Peter Pan*'s Mr Darling thought of himself as grown-up, but no one I know thinks they are.) The sections in this chapter are devoted to the kinds of experiences that are central to the process. Education, travel and work are fixed parts of the lives of most of us. Some ways of going about them will help us in the task of growing up, others will not. The central message of the last chapter – that growing up requires recognizing the gap between *is* and *ought* while trying to preserve both – means that no way of acquiring these experiences will be entirely the way it should be. The same parents who anxiously seek the ideal kindergarten for their children will usually acknowledge, not many years later, that whatever they get will be compromise. Not every compromise is rotten, of course, but to decide which ones are acceptable you must look at each case on its own.

Although 'no' is a word that toddlers learn early,

they have little choice but to accept the choices their parents made; adolescents do their best to reject every one. Growing up is a process of sifting through your parents' choices about everything: the music you couldn't help hearing because it was playing on a stereo you couldn't reach, the religion you couldn't help believing because you were taken to sermons, or holidays in a car you couldn't drive, the neighbourhood they set up home in or moved to when they changed jobs, and a host of general values you will not even recognize as values until you are old enough to get out in the world and encounter other ones. Sometimes when you're sifting, with any luck at all, you'll be able to say *that's just what I'd have chosen had I been able to choose myself,* and thank your parents for it one way or another, if only by living in a way that proves them right. On the other hand, if you don't reject any of their choices you are not grown-up – if only because their choices were made in a time that isn't this one, and not all of them fit into the world you now inhabit.

The early years of education, in particular, are up to someone else. Hannah Arendt's *Between Past and Future* contains a wonderful description of education's goal:

Education is the point at which we decide whether we love the world enough to assume responsibility for it and by the same token save it from that ruin which, except for renewal, except for the coming of the new and the young, would be inevitable. And education, too, is where we decide whether we love our children enough not to expel them from our world and leave them to their own devices, not to strike from their hands the chance of undertaking something new, something foreseen by no one, but to prepare them in advance for the task of renewing a common world. ('The Crisis in Education', in *Between Past and Future*, p. 285)

Blessed is the child who falls into the hands of more than one teacher who sees her task that way; even one can be enough to salvage the experience. For most of us, schools are something different: institutions that do a great deal to break rather than further the natural urge to explore the world that any baby's eyes reveal. (If Kant is right, those eyes reflect the Unconditioned, that idea of a world that makes sense as a whole that drives us to ask *why*.) To be sure, some of the worst parts of formal education – rote learning, corporal punishment – have been largely abolished, and some of Rousseau's ideas on education have been taken up so thoroughly that we no longer recognize them as his. In 1992 the Scottish educator John Darling wrote that the history of child-centred educational theory is a series of footnotes to Rousseau.[20] Not everyone views this as commendable, and I've argued above that even *Emile* cannot work. Still we owe to its author the idea that much of traditional education is not simply inadequate but counterproductive, killing the very desire to learn it is meant to sustain – as well as the suspicion that this death is not accidental. As Rousseau pointed out in 1763, schoolchildren who are used to sitting still while a bored teacher's jabber washes over them are unlikely, as adults, to stand up when a politician lies. Thomas Jefferson wrote that the chief political function of society is to educate its young. He may have had in mind a school system that produced active, vibrant, enlightened children, but as they are now, most schools produce docility and dull resentment. Small wonder so many children experience them as prisons.

The fact that children like Malala Yousafzai are willing to risk their lives to enter one is not simply due to the fact that forbidden fruits are the sweetest. They know that even a limited education will give them access to parts of the world that are otherwise closed. Malala is particularly admirable, but she is not entirely unique. In countries where access to schooling can be limited by a family's ability to pay for shoes or pencils, schoolbooks are treated like treasure. These facts should make those of us who live in more fortunate circumstances pause, but they should not make us complacent. Traditional schooling may be better than none at all, just as rice and beans are cherished by a child who is starving, but neither can provide the nourishment body and soul need to flourish.

Thus it's no surprise that educational reform has been a central goal of every progressive movement since the Enlightenment. This isn't a matter of improving efficiency or test scores, but of confronting the ways in which so many schools are organized to reduce human potential rather than develop it. In the most surprising of Kant's remarks on education, he takes it as given that a major function of schooling is to make us sit still.

> Children are sent to school initially not with the intention that they should already learn something there, but rather that they may grow accustomed to sitting still and observing exactly what they are told, so that in the future they may not put into practice actually and instantly each notion that strikes them.
> (*Lectures on Pedagogy*, p. 438)

As the final clause makes clear, Kant is not endorsing the practice as a means of driving the child into submission; elsewhere he inveighs against the then-common idea that education is a matter of breaking the child's will. Rather, he thinks such training important to encourage the child to develop self-discipline, for the alternative is a creature like Peter Pan, who is helplessly at the mercy of every passing whim. Children do need to be taught that not everything worth learning can be learned by following natural inclinations. Languages and music, for example, require tedious exercises that must be repeated in order to get to the point where the violin stops squeaking and the sentences no longer clunk. The exercises are not merely dull but regressive, returning us to the bare-bones achievements of earliest childhood. Even adults who cherish Peter Pan fantasies will baulk when reduced to linguistic toddlerhood – one reason why both languages and music should be learned as early as possible. (A second reason has to do with neurobiology rather than psychology, and is equally important. Our brains are shaped by experience, but never so much as in early childhood. The brain of a child who has learned a second language by the age of ten has been moulded in ways that make it much easier to learn a third or a fourth.) Children do not know the pleasures that will come with those delays of gratification, and someone needs to tell them, usually rather often. Kant sees discipline as a means to greater freedom, which is the subject of most of his discussions of education.

He was particularly interested in the work of Johann Bernhard Basedow, the German pedagogue who founded the first school in Europe that was explicitly based on Rousseau's educational principles. Opened in 1774, the Philanthropinum, Basedow's school in Dessau, was the subject of Kant's most fulsome prose:

Perhaps never before has a more just demand been made on the human race, and never before has such a great and more self-extending benefit been more unselfishly offered, than is now the case with Herr

Basedow, a man who, together with his praiseworthy
assistants, has solemnly devoted himself to the welfare and betterment of human beings.[21]

Thanks to the 'fiery and constant enthusiasm of a single astute and sprightly man', he continues, the creation
of an educational institution which is fitted to nature is
no longer a dim and distant wish but a reality. Europe
has no dearth of schools, but they were all 'spoiled at
the outset, because everything in them works against
nature, the good to which nature has given the predis-
position is far from being drawn out in the human
being'.[22] Given that traditional schools are spoiled at
the outset, Kant demands not 'slow reform but swift
revolution': the entire organization and the teachers
themselves must be transformed. For this, he believed,
nothing more was necessary than one school that was
established in a radically new way.

Kant's extravagant prose had a purpose, for Basedow's school in Dessau attracted not only his admi-
ration but his only known foray into fund-raising.
Kant's words were constructed to encourage his
audience to reach into their pockets:

We . . . look forward to numerous subscriptions,
from all gentlemen of the clerical and teaching pro-
fessions, from parents in general, to whom nothing
that serves the improved formation of their children
can be indifferent, yes even from those who, although

they do not have children, still formerly as children received an education and because of this will recognize the obligation to contribute their share, if not to the reproduction then at least to the formation of human beings. Subscriptions to the monthly publication of the Dessau Educational Institute, under the title of *Educational Treatises*, are now being accepted for 2 Reichstaler 10 Groschen of our currency. But since some additional payments might be demanded at the end of the year due to the as of yet indeterminable number of sheets, it would perhaps be best (but this is left to each person's discretion) to dedicate a Ducat, in the way of a subscription, to the furtherance of this work, whereupon the surplus is to be paid back correctly to each person who should demand it.[23]

Though fund-raising pitches look rather different nowadays, Kant's *Lectures on Pedagogy* displays a savvy concern for the relationships between funding and control. His only criticism of Basedow had to do with the school director's reliance on royal support.

For experience teaches that the princes have not so much the best for the world in mind but the well-being of their state, so that they may reach their own goals. If, however, they provide the money, then the design of the plan must be left in their hands. (*Lectures on Pedagogy*, p. 443)

Kant concludes that private funding is the best guarantee for educational transformation, since 'all culture begins with private individuals and extends outward from there' (Ibid). Like other aspects of fund-raising, private funding in Kant's day was not what it is in ours. He could not envision a world in which large businesses make large contributions to public education in order to sell their products to a quite literally captive audience. In the United States, for example, 80 percent of public high schools have signed contracts for 'pouring rights' with Coca-Cola or Pepsi, which require the schools to buy a certain amount of soda in exchange for donations that support educational activities that cash-strapped school boards cannot fund. Kant warned against the undue influence that princes might exercise on educational institutions that depended on their funding. How could he imagine that private corporations, two centuries later, might exert more subtle forms of control? It's a development of which any country that values education for some reason other than producing new consumers should beware.

Basedow never succeeded in raising enough private subscriptions to do without princely subsidies, and the Philanthropinum closed after twenty years. Basedow himself seems to have been better at conceiving educational theory than in managing a school, and left considerably earlier. But the Philanthropinum inspired a host of similar institutions across Europe and in

North America, and was reopened in Dessau after the end of the Second World War, where it exists to this day. You can find it on Facebook. Progressive schools rarely last as long as traditional ones – something usually gets lost when their original founders quit or retire – but tireless and hopeful educators and parents continue to create new ones. In this they may be sustained by Kant's thought that good education *must* be the work of generations, for we are all the products of education we did not choose, and each must work to bring posterity further than we ourselves have gone. This won't give much comfort to the parent who is leery of leaving a child in the hands of those who are unable or unwilling to keep her best interests in mind, still less to the child who is stifled and bored in too many classrooms, day after long day. Those with time and resources may choose to educate their children at home, but most of us will scrounge for the best alternative at hand. We'd prefer a school that cultivates our children's autonomy, following Kant's three principles:

1. From earliest childhood the child must be allowed to be free in all matters (except in those where it might injure itself, as, for example, when it grabs an open knife).
2. The child must be shown that it can only reach its goals by letting others also reach theirs.
3. One must prove to it that restraint is put on it in order that it may be led to the use of its

own freedom, that it is cultivated so that it
may one day be free, that is, so that it need
not depend on the care of others. (*Lectures
on Pedagogy*, pp. 447–8)

And we may agree with Kant that experiments in education are necessary in order to discover, through
experience, which methods are most suited to carry
out those principles, and that 'since experiments matter, no one generation can present a complete plan of
education' (Ibid, p. 445).

Sometimes we will see signs of progress. In many
places, methods have become more open, teachers
more attuned to children's different needs. The textbooks my children used were better than my own,
which discussed American history without even
mentioning the genocide of Native Americans, or
suggesting that girls could aspire to be much besides
mothers. But signs of progress are only useful if they
show that progress is possible, thereby sustaining our
efforts to make more. For more is absolutely necessary. Most politicians pay lip service to claims like
Kant's, for whom 'good education is exactly that from
which all the good in the world arises' (Ibid, p. 443).
But apart from notable exceptions like Finland, teachers continue to be underpaid and undervalued, and
schools continue to languish. Parents who find themselves agreeing with Kant, or simply remembering the
simmering frustration of their own school days, can

despair at their failure to offer their child the education she deserves.

They will seek the best alternative available, and do what they can to be active in improving whatever school they find. (Or found, if they're really ambitious.) They will try to offer shelter by validating some of their child's perceptions about what is going wrong in the formal education they have chosen for them. And then they'll have to face it: they are not raising Emile. Whether or not they read the book, they are likely to have begun their lives as parents gripped by its message: *nothing in the world is more important than raising a free and happy child.* Then the rest of the world kicked in. Unlike Emile's tutor, their knowledge and power are both limited – sometimes very limited, as anyone who has raised children will know. Measured by the ideals they had for their child on the day she was born, they will fail. They may take heart from British psychoanalyst D. W. Winnicott's theories. Winnicott's attention was focused on infants, for whom a perfect parent would be a problem. If the infant never experiences anxiety, she will never experience herself as an autonomous being who can act in the world. By contrast,

> The good-enough mother . . . starts off with an almost complete adaptation to her infant's needs, and as time proceeds she adapts less and less completely, gradually, according to the infant's growing ability to

deal with her failure. Her failure to adapt to every need of the child helps them adapt to external realities.[24]

Winnicott's view that the growing child *needs* to experience her parents' failings in order to gauge and develop her own strength lends weight to the criticism we saw of *Emile*. The tutor (or mother or father) who creates a world in which the child only experiences things working as they ought to will not be fit for this one. And so we might aspire to a different goal: Kant said that good parents have a duty to raise a child who is glad to have been born.

For many children, the experience of formal education is the experience where the gap between *is* and *ought* begins to yawn. Yes, there was teething, and a hundred other pains and frustrations that made no sense. But usually, it's school that presents the first institutionalized instance of dramatic conflict between the ideals that are stated and the experience that is lived. In earlier times, Jewish boys as young as three were sent to *cheder*, where they learned the Hebrew alphabet from wooden blocks dipped in honey. In today's Germany, children are given large paper cones filled with candy on their first day of school. Kant, for whom it is always a mistake to provide external rewards for something that should be done freely, would have blanched at such customs. For the children are not free, and they soon come to suspect that the sweets are meagre compensation for the bitterness of the fact that what they're told isn't true. The step into the world of education will not – or not only – help them grow and flourish; it will also stunt and wither them.

All right then: the education your parents could provide was flawed. All the more reason to take it into your own hands as soon as you can. The time of reaching legal maturity – somewhere between eighteen and twenty-one these days, though research suggests that our brains don't reach maturity until we're about twenty-five – may be the hardest time of your life. For it's the first time your choices stand in the foreground. Too much in the foreground: since it's likely to be the first time you made any significant ones, every choice has so much weight as to feel immovable. The pressure to get it all right is enormous: *this* course of study, *this* job, *this* love will determine your fate ever after. It takes another decade to learn that few mistakes are irrevocable. In the meantime, improving on the education you did not choose by making choices of your own can only be of use. Here are a few thoughts on how to do so.

Avoid places where you are the smartest person in the room, and seek out those where you aren't. This could stand as a rule for getting an education, but it doesn't always happen in schools or even universities, and it certainly shouldn't stop with them. Minds need at least as much exercise as bodies, but all too many people get stuck lifting light weights. Nor can you know in advance who has knowledge or wisdom that you might need. The smartest people I know are those who can quote classics from multiple traditions *and* learn from the astute street vendor on the corner.

About those classics: there's a reason they're still around. Invent what you like, but the wheel has been in evidence for about six millennia, and it needn't be invented again. Reading *The Republic* should make many a latter-day Thrasymachus stop short. He may have discovered something troubling, but he hasn't discovered anything new. If he wants to move the conversation about morality and power forward, he'd better know what Plato had to say about it. (At a time when so many questions about sexual relationships are up in the air he might also be interested to know that Plato banned monogamy from his ideal state, on the grounds that fathers who don't know exactly which children are theirs will be committed to raising each one.) *War and Peace* will open a window to nineteenth-century Russia, as *Middlemarch* does to nineteenth-century England, but either book will make you think differently about love and loss and integrity, and growing up with all of them. You may be an atheist, but if you never read the great texts of religion you will not understand the world's history, nor many parts of its present.

The last few decades have seen fierce debate about what is called the canon. The very word suggests ecclesiastical decree, as if a corpus of old texts were handed down by fiat, and could be ignored as soon as you've decided that authorities no longer dictate what you read. But though the canon may need to be widened, most of its contents hold up, and few things are more misguided than the attempts of some educators to appeal to their students by doing away with classic texts, often in the name of avoiding Eurocentrism. They would do better to look to the Enlightenment, often wrongly thought to be the source of Eurocentrism itself. Quite to the contrary, its authors knew how to value both universal principles and particular differences, and they knew how to tell one from the other. They were steeped in classical Western literature, though they were more likely to read Latin than Greek, but they were well aware of how much they had to learn from other cultures. Montesquieu's *Persian Letters* criticized Europe from a Muslim perspective, over Voltaire's desk hung a portrait of Confucius and Rousseau pleaded for knowledge of Africa that was not written by travellers 'more interested in filling their purses than their minds'. A grown-up relationship to your culture is no different from a grown-up relationship to your parents.

You must decide which parts of the inheritance you want to make your own – but you have to examine it first. De Beauvoir put the matter eloquently: to abandon the past is to depopulate the world.[25]

I have argued that the work of Immanuel Kant – though harder to read than that of Tolstoy or Eliot, or even Plato and Rousseau – is a bequest to be particularly cherished, though I'm well aware that some will find my emphasis not only on reading classics, but on reading at all to be out of date. Even for those of us who grew up with a love for words on pages, more reading takes place on screens these days than off them. This is not the place to survey the debate about what the internet is doing to our minds; there is much we don't know. I believe that the internet appeals to human needs for activity. When you read on the web you are not held in place by an author's intentions; you can always decide to click, click again. It's activity that can feel exhilarating, but also frenetic, and its relation to real action is no different from the relation between fast food and a warm, well-cooked stew. Reading a book demands passivity, the willingness to open yourself up to an author's design, before you use your imagination and your reason to think with her.

Plato deplored the invention of writing, which he feared would ruin our memories. How very good their memories must have been can be seen by recalling that we have no texts by Homer: *The Iliad* and *The Odyssey*, the first two great works of Western literature, are transcriptions from bards who sang them from memory centuries after they were composed. Still I'm not about to echo Plato. I spend hours most days in cyberspace, and am grateful for many of its resources; I even click on most of the links I receive from Amnesty International or Avaaz, and no longer wince at return mails that thank me for taking action. I am simply suggesting you limit your time in cyberspace, and experience action more palpable than making a cursor click. Even a week off the web can work wonders for your imagination, and your sense of being in the world.

A whole week without the internet?

When I've spoken of the good it's done me, most people have baulked. *Nice work if you can get it, but mine depends on the web.* So does much of mine. Thankfully, most of us have some form of vacation, but studies show that most of us stay connected even then. In fact, work often serves as a pretext; these days you're lucky if only half of the mail you receive is spam. For the rest of it, there are internet cafés most everywhere if you need to send a sign of life to whomever you left behind, but you needn't stay much longer than it takes to drink an espresso. This usually entails nothing worse than ignoring the magazines in your inbox that lure you with the promise of understanding something important. How often does that promise turn out to be a decoy that keeps you hooked on stories about the sleaziest romance or the most lurid crime of people you will never meet? Unless you're the foreign minister of a major country, even real news can go on without you for a while. *And my job?* If you have done it well thus far, you need not be at its mercy, and scientific investigation is hardly required to prove that the web is not only a means to productivity: honest introspection will do. But there are scientific investigations, with variations in the numbers. A recent German study estimated that we waste, on average, two working days each week writing emails that nobody needs; a recent American study concluded that 80 percent of work time spent online is unproductive; and a recent British study estimated the annual cost of cyberloafing to be billions of pounds.

Once again, just for emphasis: I'm not suggesting that we do without the web entirely, just that we refuse to let it rule. You can only find out how much it rules your life if you do without it on occasion. Doing so should leave your mind less cluttered, your thoughts more focused, and lead you to acknowledge that Rousseau's lesson still holds true: less is necessary, and more is possible, than we are ever led to believe.

Travel

But education hardly stops with book learning – or screen learning, as the case may be. To be sure, the advice to consider travel as part of an education is also advice to stay unplugged for a while. If you stay online long in Sicily you might as well stay home and look at someone else's postings.

In the fourth century of the Common Era, Augustine introduced a metaphor: 'The world is a book, and those who do not travel know only one page.' Augustine read widely, to follow his own metaphor. The man who recorded his life as a sinner and went on to become a saint was born in today's Algeria, moved on to Carthage and lived in Rome and Milan before returning to his homeland to become bishop of Hippo. It's an estimable itinerary, particularly when compared with others. Even Kant, as we saw, *wrote* that travel is a good means of broadening one's knowledge of the world, though it's hardly surprising that he wrote less enthusiastically about it than others. He also wrote that the right to visit other countries should become a condition of perpetual peace. His *Lectures on Pedagogy* suggest that schools begin with geography when teaching children, and point out that even small children are fascinated by maps.

One can't help but wonder: when reading *Emile* did he have a moment of envy? It's not an emotion we have reason to ascribe to the sage of Königsberg, though he did describe himself as a melancholic. Could he have sighed with longing when he reached Book V, where Rousseau insists that Emile must travel through Europe for two years, learn two or three of its principal languages in addition to his native one, and see everything there that is truly of interest, whether in nature, in government, in the arts or in men? For Rousseau was explicit: 'I hold it to be an incontestable maxim that whoever has seen only one people does not know men; he knows only the people with whom he has lived' (*Emile*, p. 451).

This remains as true in an era when we can watch Korean rap videos as it was in Rousseau's time. Indeed, perhaps more so: globalization gives us the illusion of knowing other cultures far better than we do. Nor is cultural ignorance confined to the less educated. I've met educated Americans who were firmly convinced that the German subway system, which doesn't require travellers to present a ticket to enter, could not possibly work (it does, relying on an honour system with occasional controls); educated Britons who couldn't imagine Nazis as ordinary people who might eat apple crumble (they did, and they also drank, slept and defecated like anyone else); educated Germans who were quite certain that Americans were incapable of understanding irony (how should an ironically functional American respond to *that*?). The fact that some of them were professors is not only a comment on the self-incurred immaturity of scholars, of whom Kant remarks

> Scholars usually are glad to allow themselves to be kept in immaturity by their wives with regard to domestic arrangements. A scholar, buried in his books,

answered the screams of a servant that there was a fire in one of the rooms: 'You know, things of that sort are my wife's affair.' (*Anthropology from a Pragmatic Point of View*, p. 104)

A less educated man might be better at putting out local fires, but he will often be just as helpless in confronting the rest of the world. What counts as rude and what counts as vulgar, which gestures are threatening and which are encouraging, what is kind and what is overbearing will likely be different from one land to the next. If you do not travel you are likely to suppose your own cultural assumptions to make up human reality – for you can only recognize what those assumptions are if you have lived in a place that runs on different ones. Travel is as important for learning about yourself and your own culture as it is for understanding others.

So Rousseau holds travel to be a crucial part of coming of age. But 'To become informed, it is not sufficient to roam through various countries. It is necessary to know how to travel' (*Emile*, p. 452). To travel simply to inform oneself is too vague an aim; young people should have a palpable interest in becoming informed. Emile is told to travel in order to study different forms of government, so that he may decide which one he wants to live under. This is not, Rousseau warns, a matter of studying 'the apparent form of a government disguised by the machinery of administration and the jargon of administrators' but of going into the country and seeing the government's effects on people's lives. (Had the aforementioned American professor observed the way subsidized public transportation actually functions in Germany he could hardly have remained convinced it was impossible.) Emile should examine the ways in which ordinary lives are affected by different political systems, so as to choose a home for his future family 'where one is always permitted to be a decent man' (Ibid, p. 457).

Rousseau is explicit not only about the goal of Emile's travels but equally about their form. Having crossed the Alps by foot himself, he was adamant that no other kind of travel is better:

> To travel on foot is to travel like Thales, Plato and Pythagoras. It is hard for me to understand how a philosopher can resolve to travel any other way and tear himself away from the examination of the riches which he tramples underfoot and which the earth lavishly offers to his sight. Who that has some liking for agriculture does not want to know the products peculiar to the climate of the places he has passed through and the way in which they are cultivated? Who that has some taste for natural history can resolve to pass by a piece of land without examining it, a boulder without chipping it, mountains without herborizing, stones without looking for fossils? . . .

I see all that a man can see, and depending only on myself, I enjoy all the liberty a man can enjoy. (Ibid, p. 412)

Other means of travelling earned Rousseau's scorn and pity; those who do not walk, sit 'sadly, like prisoners, in a small, closed-up cage'. It's a mercy he didn't live to witness the railroad that shocked later generations. In an 1837 letter the French writer Victor Hugo described a train journey:

The flowers at the edge of the field are no longer flowers but specks of colour, or rather red and white stripes; there are no longer any points at all, just streaks; the cities, the church towers, and the trees perform a dance mixed up in a crazy way with the horizon. (Quoted in Wolfgang Schivelbusch, *Geschichte der Eisenbahnreise*, p. 54)

Hugo was not alone. Countless numbers of his contemporaries complained that train journeys had made the landscape evaporate. By the mid-nineteenth century, a means had been found to compensate travellers for the railways' unnerving speed: the book. W. H. Smith received its first concession to sell books in London's Euston Station in 1848. The assumption that trains are good for reading (as well as the proliferation of station bookstores) quickly spread across

Europe – in order to politely avoid conversation with other passengers as well as to console for the loss of landscape that disturbed Hugo, and would have inflamed Rousseau. It's interesting to imagine what they would have said about easyJet.

Rousseau was not the last philosopher to cross swathes of Europe by foot. Simone de Beauvoir did it often, both with and without Sartre, and her descriptions of the experience are as rapturous as Rousseau's. In 1934, for example, she

> walked solidly for three weeks, keeping away from main roads and taking short cuts through woods and fields. Every peak was a challenge. Eagerly my eyes drank in the magnificent scenery – lakes, waterfalls, hidden gorges and valleys. I carried all my possessions on my back, I had no idea where I would sleep each night, and I was still on the move when the first star pierced the sky . . . Often I could not bear the thought of being cut off from grass and trees and sky: at least I wanted to keep their scent with me. So instead of taking a room in the inn, I would trudge on another four or five miles and beg hospitality in some hamlet, and the smell of hay would drift through my dreams. (*The Prime of Life*, p. 217)

I can't shake a feeling somewhere between envy and melancholy when reading such lines, or de Beauvoir's descriptions of exploring the Colosseum in the

Roman starlight, seeking traces of Shakespeare and Dickens in London, playing Greek music on the deck of a boat from Santorini. Their journeys were frequent, long, and intensive in ways that are nearly impossible to replicate now. Those journeys, said Sartre, not only made him wild with delight; they gave him an extra dimension.[26] Such travel undoubtedly brings you closer to everything you left home to see, be it the glories of the natural world or the curiosities of those who people it. But the Colosseum was jammed last time I saw it, and it's hard to find places where you could walk for three weeks without running into barriers (or shotguns, if you tried to do so in some parts of the United States). Several northern European countries guarantee the right to roam with few restrictions; Scotland, Norway and Estonia are among the nations whose laws protect public access to land. But with increasingly less of it available, and increasingly more travellers to share it with, few of us will be able to imitate Rousseau and de Beauvoir even if we're so inclined. Travel on foot, like Rousseau's second-best option, travel on horseback, largely belongs to the past.

By contrast, Rousseau's description of the wrong way to travel feels remarkably contemporary. Travel is a crucial part of Emile's education, but it isn't right for everyone. For those who are missing the openness and powers of observation that Emile's education provided, travel can be worse than useless:

What makes it still more unfruitful for young people is the way they are made to do it. Governors, who are more interested in their own entertainment than in their pupils' instruction, lead them from city to city, from palace to palace, from social circle to social circle; or if the governors are learned and men of letters, they make their pupils spend their time roaming libraries, visiting antique shops, going through old monuments and transcribing old inscriptions . . . The result is that, after having roamed Europe at great expense, abandoned to frivolities or boredom, they return without having seen anything which can interest them or learned anything which can be useful to them. (*Emile*, p. 468)

This could serve as a comment on most of the thousands of university programmes that send young people abroad with the promise of learning in and from another culture, and keep them in conditions under which they cannot possibly do so. They are given just enough language training to allow them to order a beer or a bread loaf, taught other subjects by (usually underpaid and often underqualified) instructors in their own language, and kept busily separate from all but chance encounters with the young people of the country in which they are staying. The cocoon thus created is far tighter than the one they inhabited at home. Even in the protected environment of an American college, the student's native cultural competence permits her to have a conversation with a baker or a bartender that could bring her into contact with a wider world, or get a job as a waitress that will teach her even more. Not every student will take advantage of those opportunities, but the typical foreign exchange student does not have them at all. She returns from Rome or Paris worse off than when she left, for she is likely to believe that she was given the foreign experience the university advertised – when she was simply transferred from one cloister to another. The vague sense of disappointment she may feel on her return will likely be felt as another disappointment with the world itself, which turned out to be no different than what she already knew. For there it is on her CV: she has lived in France.

Travel is meant to help us come of age, but it often turns out to be another form of infantilization. This is just as true of most adult ways of travelling. The American philosopher George Santayana was generous in writing:

> The latest type of traveler, and the most notorious, is the tourist. Having often been one myself, I will throw no stones at him; from the tripper off on a holiday to the eager pilgrim thirsting for facts or for beauty, all tourists are dear to Hermes, the god of travel, who is patron also of amiable curiosity and freedom of mind. There is wisdom in turning as

often as possible from the familiar to the unfamiliar: it keeps the mind nimble, it kills prejudice, and it fosters humor.[27]

Born in Spain to a diplomatic family, the multilingual Santayana would have been a rather different tourist than most. Even more important, he wrote these lines at the turn of the last century. In 2012, the World Tourist Organization counted 1.035 *billion* foreign tourists. Most of them travel in groups with their country-folk, shepherded by guides who rush them through a list that consists less of sights to be seen than of backdrops for photographs, before depositing them at shops whose wares they could have bought at home. It's an experience that positively precludes real encounters with the country they are visiting, for the very sight of such a group causes native inhabitants to depart – unless they have something to sell them, hiding snickers with smiles just long enough for money to change hands. *Pace* Santayana, it's hard to imagine such tourists are any dearer to Hermes than they are to the people whose capitals they clog.

Mass tourism presents a democratic veneer, allowing millions at least a glimpse of the experiences that were formerly restricted to people of privilege. But travel is not about glimpsing, and only partly about seeing; it's a matter of keeping all your senses open to other ways of being in the world. Nor is it only mass tourism that prevents the experience it professes to offer. Any honest traveller annoyed by the mobs that prevent her from being alone with Michelangelo or bartering in a souk will admit that she's part of the problem. For those for whom a modicum of wealth or fame provide the access, there are ways of travelling that are more exclusive and less noisy, but they rarely provide insight into anything foreign. David Lodge's brilliant descriptions of scientific conferences could apply with minor changes to international art fairs, psychoanalytic congresses, or the world economic forum at Davos.

Whheeeeee! Europe, here we come! Or Asia, or America, or wherever. It's June, and the conference season is well and truly open. The whole academic world seems to be on the move. Half the passengers on transatlantic flights these days are university teachers. Their luggage is heavier than average, weighed down with books and papers – and bulkier, because their wardrobes must embrace both formal wear and leisure wear, clothes for attending lectures in, and clothes for going to the beach in, or to the Museum, or the Schloss, or the Duomo, or the Folk Village. For that's the attraction of the conference circuit: it's a way of converting work into play, combining professionalism with tourism, and all at someone else's expense. Write a paper and see the world! I'm Jane Austen – fly

me! Or Shakespeare, or T. S. Eliot, or Hazlitt. All
tickets to ride, to ride the jumbo jets. *Wheeeeeee!* (*Small
World*, p. 231)

Such tours are better packaged: the guardians more
deferential, the sights more exceptional and the food
assuredly better than what's offered by student
exchange programmes or mass excursions, but the
packaging remains. Hence they feed even bigger illusions (*If some institution or other is willing to pay for me to get
from here to there, aren't I really a grown-up now?*) while
doing little more to expand the experience of new
worlds.

Nostalgia isn't helpful, though it would be stupid to
deny that we have lost a part of the world we should
have tried harder to keep. With one-sixth of the
world's population choosing to be on the move,
travel cannot be what it was in earlier times. No doubt
eighteenth-century travellers had other causes for
worry besides crowds – that is, other travellers – like
the highwaymen who appear when the roads are
empty. Still it's hard not to miss the days when travellers were fewer and less guarded, their destinations
bare of branches of multinational corporations bent
on making every place look like every other. Then
again, not every eighteenth-century traveller was able
to see the unfamiliar. Despite a considerable amount
of time spent in a France that was far more different
from his Britain than it is to ours, Hume could write:

Should a traveller, returning from a far country, bring us an account of men, wholly different from any with whom we were ever acquainted . . . we should immediately, from these circumstances, detect the falsehood, and prove him a liar, with the same certainty as if he had stuffed his narration with stories of centaurs and dragons. (*Enquiry concerning Human Understanding*, p. 84)

Wholly different from any with whom we were ever acquainted. But that's just what you travel to find out. Are we moved by the same passions, do we have the same dreams? Are there universal principles of human nature? Differences that do not translate? Every good traveller is a nascent anthropologist, seeking to understand what is similar and what is distinct in peoples and cultures. The only feasible way for mortals to do so is to spend real time in one or preferably two cultures that are significantly different from their own. (Two are more than twice as good as one. If you have only lived in one foreign country, you'll be inclined to split the world into two ways of being, and seesaw forever between them. Living in a third brings home the idea that there are many ways to diverge.) Global capitalism has reduced cultural contrasts, but it hasn't erased them. To watch a German waiting for a McDonald's on Berlin's Alexanderplatz and an American in the same queue is to see all the differences: how the German orders, how the American stands, how they count their change and take their bags and depart with their friends is to see how much culture remains even where it might seem lost.

Living in another culture means working in it, preferably not in the foreign branch of your current employer. Diplomats are usually transferred every few years to prevent their going native. I'm suggesting, by contrast, that you do so, as far as it's humanly possible. Working lets you learn what tourists cannot know. For taking responsibility and avoiding it, how goals are set and tasks divided, what is collective and what is independent all look somewhat different in different cultures. None of those are things that can be learned quickly. It requires at the very least a year, which also gives you a sense of the rhythm of seasons, and how differently changes of light and heat and foliage change ordinary lives. Ideally you should live in a place that requires you to learn a language that is not your mother tongue, for every language conveys presumptions that are concealed until compared with another one. How do you think about gender in a language where all the objects have one, or where none of them do? What about all the verbs? How do you deal with intimacy in a language that addresses people differently according to distance, or with hierarchies when it distinguishes according to age? What to do when you find their form of expression to be ponderous or flowery, and they find yours to be rude?

The Austrian philosopher Ludwig Wittgenstein

wrote: 'A philosophical problem has the form: *I don't know my way about.*'[28] Travelling wisely preserves just this state, and part of the reason it helps in growing up is that it requires a return to positions you left as a child. You do not know how far your standing – your success at school or work, your place in a family or a town – keeps you grounded until you give it up. You will smile and nod too often at all the things you do not understand. You will be helpless before tasks that once seemed so easy you never stopped to reflect how many kinds of competence they require. You will feel overwhelmed and lonely, and you may find comfort in the French philosopher Camus's remark that what gives value to travel is fear. You will also feel the small child's wonder at the most everyday pieces of your new world, for the trash bins on the road to Marrakesh and the trees on the streets of Odessa reveal stories about the people who live, and lived there. (Substitute, at random, your favourite points of wonder.) But you will likely conclude – as Kant said of Adam and Eve, on some accounts the world's first travellers – that however comfortable it was to stay in the garden, the departure from home was the first step to freedom, and thence to progress. Like any departure, it is also a loss.

It's easy to hear the grumble: *this is all very well for those who can afford it, but few people have the means for that kind of travel.* Neither Rousseau nor the young de Beauvoir could afford to travel in style, and each of them told stories of being stuck in foreign towns without a sou, dining on bread and onions or sleeping in abandoned huts. Travelling without money is one thing the internet has made easier since their days. If you're willing to work for food and lodging, you can pick tea in India, teach Ugandan orphans to dance, staff the office of a chocolate factory in Guatemala, plant grapes in Albania, dig with archaeologists in Siberia, construct sustainable farms in Morocco. Those looking for tamer stuff can care for the very young or very old in Cornwall, or tend a restaurant garden in southern France. These are a fraction of the possibilities found in a few minutes' search of a single website, and they are open to people of any age. All it costs is a ticket to get there and the decision to reject the voices that tell you such journeys are impossible. Perhaps they do not want you to understand where you came from: for that's the greatest gift that travel will give you.

Work

For the ancient philosophers, work was something done by slaves or women, and therefore not worthy of interest. Despite the many differences between them, both Plato and Aristotle believed that a life devoted to contemplation was the highest form of living. One hallmark of modernity was a reversal of this value: not contemplation but activity came to be seen as most fundamentally human. Chalk it up, if you like, to changing conceptions of property. John Locke was the first philosopher to write seriously about labour. His *Second Treatise of Government*, published in 1689, asked how private property can be justified if the Bible tells us that God gave the earth to humankind in common. His answer was simple: even in the state of nature we own our bodies, and if we mix the labour of our bodies with something, we own that thing too. The farmer who tills the earth, plants a seed, tends a sapling and harvests its fruits has every right to have them – as long as he only takes as much as he can eat before they rot, and leaves enough and as good for others. It's such a sweet account of private property that Rousseau sets Emile to plant a bean patch in order to understand it. But Locke's conditions on accumulation were circumvented by the invention of money, which unlike plums or apples, never rots, and it's been argued that Locke's theory was actually developed in order to justify early capital accumulation. Contemporary industrialists are happy to use the view to argue for lower taxes, as if founding a company (dependent on workers who actually make things as well as the schools that train them and the roads they use to reach the factory, not to mention the police who keep others from stealing it) were equivalent to working one's own little plot of land. But for all the ways in which Locke's labour theory of property may be inadequate it did have the advantage of moving labour to centre stage.

For Kant it is action that gives life meaning, so much so that action becomes a duty. His *Foundation of the Metaphysics of Morals* considers a rich man who has no need to work and is inclined to let his talents rust and give his life over to idleness, amusement and pro-creation 'like the South Sea islanders'. Should he do it, Kant says, he would neglect his duty to his own humanity, since he, like the rest of us, was born with faculties that were made to be developed.

> Just as false is the idea that if Adam and Eve had only remained in paradise they would have done nothing there but sit together, sing arcadian songs, and observe the beauty of nature. Certainly boredom would have tortured them just as much as it does other people in a similar situation. The human being must be so occupied that he is filled with the purpose that he has before his eyes, in such a way that he is not conscious of himself at all, and the best rest for him is one that comes after work. (*Lectures on Pedagogy*, p. 461)

Hegel's paean to labour went considerably further. In his account of the epic struggle for recognition with which the consciousness of our own humanity begins, work has the upper hand. History, in Hegel's *Phenomenology of Spirit* (1807), begins with a battle in which the defeated man becomes the other's slave. But the master's triumph is short-lived, for the slave who is forced to work for him is actually doing something, which makes him the motor that pushes world-history forward. Indeed in giving form to matter, he's the living image of God. Hegel's dialectic was the starting point for Marx's view that our capacity to work is what distinguishes us from animals, making us the creative beings we project onto the heavens. A few higher animals do make occasional products, but only humans produce the means of production themselves. Thus the alienation of labour – the fact that most of us sell our capacity to labour to someone who owns the means of production – not only deprives workers of the fruits of their labour by paying them 1/200th of the salary that goes to their CEO (the international average as of this writing, not including bonuses and stock options); it deprives workers of the very meaning of labour itself – that human activity that makes us free of nature, hence almost divine. In a truly human society, Marx thought all our capacities to work would develop: we would hunt in the morning, fish in the afternoon and do philosophy after dinner.

Arendt was so convinced that activity is essential to being human that she gave her book *The Human Condition* a Latin title: *Vita Activa*. She ties activity to natality, which we saw she viewed as the central category of political thought:

Labor assures not only individual survival, but the life of the species. Work and its product, the human artifact, bestow a measure of permanence and durability upon the futility of mortal life and the fleeting character of human time. Action, in so far as it engages in founding and preserving political bodies, creates the condition for remembrance, that is, for history. Labor and work, as well as action, are also rooted in natality insofar as they have the task to provide and preserve the world for, to foresee and reckon with, the constant influx of newcomers who are born into the world as strangers. (*The Human Condition*, pp. 8–9)

Arendt wanted to make the general Enlightenment claims about human activity more specific, and criticized Marx, in particular, for failing to distinguish between labour and work. Labour is the sort of thing we do of necessity, the repetitive production of – chiefly edible – goods that we need to survive. It is never entirely free, for its demands are made by nature, nor does it produce anything that lasts. Work, by contrast, is the activity that has the free and divine qualities glimpsed by Hegel and Marx. For work is the creation of lasting objects, from tables to artworks, that create a world that allows us to determine a place in the universe that would otherwise be as inconstant and impermanent as we are. Very early, we learn we will perish:

The task and potential greatness of mortals lie in their ability to produce things – works and deeds and words – which would deserve to be, and at least to a degree, are at home in everlastingness, so that through them mortals could find a place in a cosmos where everything is immortal except themselves. (Ibid, p. 19)

You do not need philosophy to see that work that transforms some piece of the world is central to being human. Watching a toddler make mud-pies might be enough. She is so very serious. Children begin to make things as soon as they've gained sufficient control of their fingers to hold a shovel or a crayon, and will do so without stopping unless they're put in front of one or another transfixing screen. In Margaret Mead's Samoa, and in poor countries around the world, children as young as five are expected to labour at tasks that make real contributions to their families' lives. In the developed world, work is the province of adults, indeed the paradigmatic activity of adulthood. You may drop out of school, you may never yearn to travel, but learning how to work is crucial to growing up.

So it's not surprising that Rousseau devoted a considerable amount of thought to it. (No, we are not entirely done with Rousseau, who will shadow us anywhere we go with Kant. This fact by itself should give the lie to those who caricature Kant as a soulless, rule-driven formalist.) Rousseau worked as an engraver's apprentice, a servant, a sign painter, a secretary and a music teacher until literary success, and the ensuing noble patronage, allowed him to live by his pen. His fictitious Emile is born into property, so nothing compels him to work for a living. But Rousseau is adamant that he owes others more than he would were he born without property, since he was so favoured at birth. Since no father can transmit to his son the right to be useless to others, anyone who eats in idleness what he does not earn himself is no better than a brigand.

> Outside of society isolated man, owing nothing to society, has a right to live as he pleases. But in society, where he necessarily lives at the expense of others, he owes them the price of his keep in work. This is without exception. To work is therefore an indispensable duty for man. Rich or poor, powerful or weak, every idle citizen is a rascal. (*Emile*, p. 195)

Thus Emile is to learn a trade. He already knows how to cultivate the land; Rousseau had him plant a bean patch not only to give him a tangible lesson on Locke's theory of property, but to make sure he could grow his own food. But the farmer is subject to vicissitudes of fortune, be it bad weather, war, or a lawsuit that takes away his field. The artisan, by contrast, can go where he will. He has no need to fear or flatter. As

long as he can create things of value, he will be fed
and he will be free.

> 'A trade for my son! My son an artisan! Sir, are you in
> your right mind?' I am thinking clearly, more clearly
> than you, madame, who wants to reduce him to never
> being able to be anything but a lord, a marquess, a
> prince, and perhaps one day less than nothing. I want
> to give him a rank which he cannot lose, a rank which
> does him honor at all times. (Ibid, p. 196)

Rousseau considers a number of trades before set-
tling on carpentry. It is clean, it is useful, it can even be
elegant, and it keeps the body strong while requiring
diligence and skill. Best of all, since carpentry is a
trade that will always fill genuine needs, it is entirely
independent of false ones, and the dependence they
create and require.

> You are an architect or a painter. So be it. But you have
> to make your talent known. Do you think you can just
> start out by showing a work at the Salon? Oh, that is
> not the way it goes! You have to belong to the Acad-
> emy. You even have to have pull in it in order to obtain
> some obscure place in the corner. Leave your ruler and
> brush, I tell you. Take a cab and run from door to door.
> It is thus that celebrity is acquired . . . Count on its
> being more important to be a charlatan than a capable
> man if the only trade you know is your own. (Ibid)

This is, Rousseau notes, just as true of those who intend to teach, work as political advisers, or fill most of the positions that confer any status at all today. Most parents still prefer that their children learn to work with words or numbers – preferably the latter – than with their hands, never realizing that this is likely to keep them in positions of permanent dependence. A trade, by contrast, may allow them to triumph over fortune itself. Rousseau's advice remains wise, even if today's Emiles are less likely to stand in rustic back-yard sheds than in workshops filled with power saws so loud they're required to wear earplugs. They will always be able to earn their living where they choose. If you can build a table or fix a house, there are people in Provence or Tonga who'd be glad to hear from you.

Rousseau was not alone in taking carpentry as a paradigm for honest, useful work. Arendt's discussion of work versus labour mentions tables rather often. But the world doesn't need *that* many tables; not everyone can follow Emile's example. And today's advice to learn multiple, portable skills will be less likely to focus on the satisfaction that you gain when you cultivate all your talents and the freedom you enjoy when you exercise them, and more on the spectre of unemployment. For we have other problems. Rousseau introduced the idea of false needs, and showed how the systems we live in work against our growing up: they dazzle us with toys and bewilder us with so many trivial products that we are too busy making silly choices to remember that the adult ones are made by others. These ideas are still subversive, important and worth repeating. But things have got worse than the most prescient eighteenth-century thinker could have imagined.

Paul Goodman described the problem more than fifty years ago. While Goodman too accepted the Enlightenment's 'philosophical truth that except in worthwhile activity there is no way to be happy', his *Growing Up Absurd* argued that what troubles adolescents is the fact that there is no decent work to grow up for (p. 45). Grown-up work would be unquestionably useful, and it would require energy, spirit and the use of our best capacities; work, that is, that can be done with honour and dignity. Fewer jobs than ever meet these criteria; most involve doing things that are patently useless, possibly harmful, certainly wasteful and demeaning and dumb to boot. And Goodman was writing in an era of full employment; these days millions of qualified young people are glad to find any job at all. Their choices are often worse than those available to young people in Goodman's day. Those who choose manual labour are likely to find themselves making products that are designed to fail. Those with verbal skills may go into teaching, a notably honourable calling, but are likely to find themselves ground down by educational institutions that undermine the very goals they claim to serve. The rest are likely to end up as salespeople, business managers or advertisers.

Goodman's scorn for the latter is especially chilling. His focus is not on the economic and political problem of the synthetic demand created by advertisements 'but the human problem that [the actors] are human beings working as clowns; that the writers and designers of it are human beings thinking like idiots; and the broadcasters and underwriters know and abet what goes on. Alternately, they are liars, confidence men, smooth talkers, obsequious, or insolent' (*Growing Up Absurd*, p. 32).

Advertising has become more subtle and ubiquitous since Goodman wrote, so that we are less aware of its impact, and liable to forget that it was not always part of the landscape. One of Henry James's last novels predicts that 'the new science' of advertising will change the world. A hundred years later we no longer perceive these changes, nor the ways in which advertising invades our lives. Perhaps the only way to do so is to spend time in a place, like Cuba, where it's absent. Landing in Havana you notice at once the absence of billboards, and you no longer need consider whether the studied contortions they depict are clever or silly. Suddenly you're aware of questions you ask yourself elsewhere: *is it better than what I've got? Will it look like that on me? Make him happy? Make her envious? Can I get there before the sale ends?* Those questions arise on the thin edge of consciousness. Somewhere underneath it, advertising entangles emotion. The models it pictures are sleek, and impossibly hot. They are meant to make your self-assurance crumble. *If I had one of those, could I ever look as stunning? If I had one of that, could I snag another heart?* The fact that the advertising industry uses the term 'creatives' to designate people who spend their lives seeking new ways of seeping into our brains in order to convince us to buy things we don't need is just the cherry on top of a travesty.

Without better models of adult work that is meaningful, our reluctance to grow up is hardly surprising. Goodman asks us to be astonished at facts we've come to take for granted: most of us no longer have the luxury of asking whether a job is genuinely productive, but only whether it pays well and has tolerable conditions. *'The question is what it means to grow up into such a fact as: during my productive years I will spend eight hours a day doing what is no good'* (Ibid, p. 35, original italics). These conditions make no sense, yet we have come to believe that they are naturally a part of the way the world is. Or the way the world was; in an era of weakened unions, declining wages and permanent electronic availability, most of us would be glad if only *eight* hours of our day were devoted to something senseless.

There are many ways in which work has become harder and less satisfying over the last century, but I will focus on one. Goodman and other critics of his generation mentioned planned obsolescence, and the foregoing discussion of philosophies of work should allow us to understand what a horror it is. Many oppressive features of the social world arose without deliberate design, making conspiracy theories look silly, but this one was actually the work of a cartel. In 1924 the Phoebus Cartel, an association of manufacturers including General Electric, Osram and Philips, held a meeting in Switzerland. They agreed to reduce the life of light bulbs – at the time proudly averaging 2,500 hours, though light bulbs exist that have burned for 100 years – to 1,000 hours, thereby more than doubling the number of light bulbs that would be sold. Members of the cartel controlled their subsidiaries firmly, and those who did not reduce the quality of their light bulbs were fined. The cartel was successful, within a decade, in making the thousand-hour light bulb the standard. But it probably required no conspiracy; the idea was in the air. In 1928 the young advertising journal *Printers Ink* proclaimed 'an article that refuses to wear out is a tragedy for business'. The manufacture of goods designed to decay was hardly limited to light bulbs. The auto industry discovered it early, allowing General Motors to dominate the market by 1931, edging out Henry Ford, who clung to the obsolete idea that goods should be built to last.

The phrase 'planned obsolescence' was first used in a pamphlet written in 1932 by American entrepreneur Bernard London, who argued that in order to reduce unemployment during the Great Depression, the government should make planned obsolescence compulsory. In an age that had yet to develop environmental concerns, the solution looked simple: the more often a product decays, the more products need to be made, the more workers needed to make them. There was no need to be explicit about the greater profit created for corporations. London's proposal for compulsory planned obsolescence proved unnecessary, for the advertising industry was learning that seduction was more effective than legal force. Convincing consumers that their things were unfashionable before they actually broke down began in the 1950s in earnest. Occasionally a product still needed tinkering: after DuPont invented nylon stockings strong enough to tow a truck, it sent its chemists back to the laboratory to design ones that ran when snagged by a fingernail. Today's products often hide computer chips that ensure their demise, and we now expect to replace most of the things we depend on every few years. Nor does the maintenance of this system of production any longer require cartels or fines. In 1981, the East German light-bulb manufacturer whose products lit up half Beijing tried to peddle its longer-lasting wares at a West German trade fair. No company was interested in stocking them. The factory was closed shortly after the fall of the Berlin Wall ended travel restrictions for Eastern Europeans, and business restrictions for Western companies.

Critics as different as Goodman, Vance Packard

and David Riesman deplored the introduction of planned obsolescence, and other features of the burgeoning consumer culture of the early 1960s. That's probably the reason the term went out of use and was replaced by the woollier 'product life cycle'. Life cycles sound normal, part of an organic process of birth and decay. We now find it natural that most of the objects we use will need replacement before we have finished paying for them. Arendt's analysis reveals just how unnatural this assumption is:

> Without taking things out of nature's hands and consuming them, and without defending himself against the natural processes of growth and decay, the laboring animal could not survive. But without being at home in the midst of things whose durability makes them fit for use and for erecting a world whose very permanence stands in direct contrast to life, this life would never be human. (*The Human Condition*, p. 135)

Arendt's account in *The Human Condition* extends and refines modern philosophy's conviction that human life is not passive. To use another sort of language, we are formed in the image of the Creator, a Being who could make a *world*. Contemporary life turns this upside down, for it is based on an economy that is not only vastly unequal, and destructive to the planet; it undermines the fundamental human value itself, the desire to create something of value. We want our labours to bear fruits that have nothing to do with paying the rent. Sometimes you can see it: the satisfaction on the face of a craftsman who wants to carve a table, cobble a shoe, form a sentence, bake a loaf that will last. (Since the loaf cannot last without getting mouldy, Arendt would demote its production to the realm of labour rather than work. Still a great baker wants you to remember the taste of that loaf after it's gone.) But though not a few young people are returning to the world of craftsmanship, the very word 'craft' has become associated with 'hobby', something done as diversion by young children or Alzheimer's patients precisely because they produce nothing of value. Words often mask even more than they reveal.

Why do grown-ups want to produce something of value? Call it an act of gratitude: we want to give something back to the world as thanks for the gift of having lived in it. You could also call it narcissism: the desire to leave a mark on the world. The two may come together as a part of our sense of dignity: as this particular human being I want to put something in the world, with a signature. *This is some of who I am.* (As Arendt noted, part of the curse of slavery is to pass through the world with no trace of having existed in it.) That dignity is negated in an economy that is driven by the production of junk. Products designed to rapidly become waste are usually called by other names, but it is telling that the world's highest-earning business sector, the financial industry, succeeded in calling a product 'junk bonds' and has yet to be punished for the wasteland it left behind.

Some words have become more explicit, and some more obscuring, since criticisms like these were made in the 1950s, when Goodman could describe this vision of the future as exaggerated:

Conceive that the man-made environment is now *out* of human scale. Business, government, and real property have now closed up *all* the space there is . . . Public speech quite disregards human facts. There is a rigid caste system in which every one has a slot and the upper group stands for nothing culturally. The university has become merely a training ground for technicians and cultural anthropologists . . . The FBI has a file card of all the lies and truths about everybody. And so forth. (*Growing Up Absurd*, p. 123)

We may envy his fears. They would have been preferable to the world we have come, fifty years later, to take as given. There is so little space left that what began as protest against these conditions – think rock 'n' roll and blue jeans – became commercial opportunities, and the internet that was meant to connect and liberate us has connected us, all right, to forms of surveillance of which Goodman's FBI could only dream. Still there are many for whom the connections do liberate, enabling groups of critical activists to form international bonds to act in concert against these conditions. Some have become active in order to save the planet. They are not wrong in thinking that this is the condition on everything else we may want, but many environmental activists have misplaced the blame. It's easy to find denunciations that blame the Enlightenment for climate change, for example, because it valorized restless acting upon, rather than peaceful coexistence with nature. Such denunciations endorse a return to earlier ways of living, often valorizing pre-Enlightenment cultures.

Others see a larger picture: our current condition is not the fulfilment of Enlightenment attitudes but the subversion of them. The behaviour that is threatening life on earth is a perversion of everything life should be. We are born with the urge for a life that embraces every kind of activity, be it learning or travel or work. Yet we're both caught and complicit in a world that turns human needs upside down. The problem is not the grown-up recognition that reality never quite matches the ideals we have for it. It's far worse, and more systemic, than that. We tell children that all the questions they ask, and many they've yet to think of, will be answered in school, and we send them to institutions that will dull their desire to pose questions at all. We want to find out more about the world than can be found in any one piece of it, but our travels are mostly regressions: either touring under conditions more protected than anything we experience in the adult world, or escaping from it altogether – otherwise known as playing in the sunniest heap of sand you can afford. We want to make an impact on the world, but we end up making or selling playthings that are developed to keep us distracted and designed to deconstruct. We have turned the activities that were meant to be the stuff of life into mere means of subsisting in it. In sum: the ways of life we have learned to take for granted are a twisted inversion of life itself. Who wants to grow up to that?

I've been using philosophy to show something about the conceptual horror of the world we have come to, in the hope that understanding the depth of its violation of our own natures will be of use in acting against it, but none of the facts I mention is new. They are so screamingly apparent that the German writer Ingo Schulze compares those who express thoughts like these to the child in Hans Christian Andersen's story 'The Emperor's New Clothes'.[29] Everyone knows that the rulers stand naked, but nobody cares to say it – for fear of no punishment greater than being called childish or dumb. (*Perhaps it's just me who fails to understand the necessary complexities of financial markets?*) Schulze was amazed when the financial crisis revealed policies far worse than anything he'd been taught about capitalism in school – sometime in the 1970s, in communist East Germany.

What happened in 1989 affected far more than Eastern Europe. The sight of thousands streaming through the Berlin Wall seemed to make any comparison of the two systems beside the point. Since the end of the Cold War, neo-liberalism – the view that free unregulated markets producing ever-increasing amounts of shoddy goods are the basis of human happiness – has assumed not merely religious but absolutist tones. Those who seek alternatives are glibly dismissed as old hippies or closet Stalinists, and Margaret Thatcher's famous statement – *there is no alternative* – is accepted even by those who think: *that cannot be right.* It cannot be an accident that evolutionary psychology, which predicates natural and constant competition as the basis of human action, became the most popular explanation of human behaviour at just the same time.

It is certainly not an accident that religious fundamentalism exploded at the same moment when market fundamentalism became the leading global ideology, though it is a tragedy that it has become the most popular alternative to it. The winners of the Cold War were certain that other ideologies would be replaced by their own neo-liberalism, in which the bottom line is the measure of all value. Against such predictions, the past decades have witnessed the rage in rejection of the idea that material needs are what move us, and everything else is expendable fluff. That idea was succinctly attacked by Marx long ago:

The bourgeois . . . has drowned the most heavenly ecstasies of religious fervour . . . in the icy water of egotistical calculation. It has resolved personal worth into exchange value, and in place of the numberless indefeasible chartered freedoms has set up that single, unconscionable freedom – Free Trade . . . All that is solid melts into air, all that is holy is profaned. (*Manifesto of the Communist Party*, 1848)

But at a time when every promise of Marxism seemed undermined by the failures of real existing socialism, the shortest road to idealism was traditional religion. Every serious study of jihadis confirms that the bitterest opponents of contemporary Western culture are those who had some access to it.[30] Osama bin Laden was not revered for his organization – far less powerful, and more chaotic, than often assumed – but for the fact that he scorned all the things his vast wealth could buy him and went off to live in a cave.

Fundamentalism has been on the rise in all major religions, for it seems to offer something of value that cannot be bought or sold. Even where it does not lead to violence, its tragedy is its inability to offer the kind of dignity it seeks. There is nothing grown-up about behaviour that's dictated by religious authority. But what alternatives do we offer? A world in which former mayor Rudy Giuliani's idea of an uplifting – no, heroic – response to the terrorist attack on New York was to tell its citizens to go shopping, is a world that has incorporated a slogan once meant to be ironic: *whoever dies with the most toys wins.* Where children can no longer see that growing up has more meaning than increasing your collection of playthings, some will look for the simplest substitute at hand.

Fortunately, in the past several years, other people have begun to develop alternatives. None of them are as yet mass movements, but small groups determined to find other means of production and consumption, labour and work, are arising all over the globe. They are committed to determining the world, not simply being determined by it, to consume some things wisely rather than being consumed by them. It doesn't take great insight to see that our present conditions are unfit for grown-up human beings. If Schulze's parable is right, it takes no insight at all, just the courage not to fear that the truths that need to be spoken will be dismissed as childish. But is anything less grown-up than worrying about whether others think you are?

4. Why Grow Up?

The short answer is: because it's harder than you think, so hard that it can amount to resistance. The forces that shape our world are no more interested in real grown-ups than they were in Kant's day, for children make more compliant subjects (and consumers). In pointing this out Kant was careful to point out the ways in which we collude in our own immaturity: thinking for yourself is less comfortable than letting someone do it for you. While the structure of the problem was already clear to Kant, the means by which we are kept in states of immaturity are more subtle and invasive than they once were. We're besieged by mixed messages. Half of them urge us to get serious, stop dreaming and accept the world as it is, promoting the picture of adulthood as capitulation to the status quo. The other half blasts us with products and suggestions that are meant to keep us young. What we rarely receive is a picture of adulthood that represents it as the ideal it should be. If the dismal vision of maturity was never explicitly planned by those whose interests lie in the world remaining no better than it is now, it serves those interests well. What better way to keep people in self-incurred immaturity than presenting a vision of maturity to which no right-minded soul could aspire?

What do you think of when you hear the word 'serious'? The dictionaries are double-edged. They list synonyms like *stern, unsmiling, grim, dour* and *humourless*, but also *earnest, genuine, wholehearted, committed, resolute*. 'Meaning what one says or does' is one definition; 'concerned with grave, important or complex matters' is another. The dominant picture of adulthood blends all these meanings into one sour brew. As a result, even very thoughtful people can take the resolution not to grow up as a sign of freedom and spirit – as I discovered in the reactions of two friends upon hearing I was writing this book. Each of them, differently, is among the most successful grown-ups I know, though only one has achieved anything resembling conventional success. Both are grandfathers now, still leading lives of passionate work as artists and authors, of open-hearted multilingual travel and activism. Both were dismayed, and one was disgusted, on hearing my choice of theme. The other said bluntly: 'My hero was always Peter Pan.' You'd never guess it if you met him.

Given the complexity of social forces arrayed against it, coming of age is a subversive ideal. Like any ideal, it can guide our actions, but it will never be fully realized by any of them. Rousseau's problem remains with us: it's impossible to create fully active and responsible citizens in a society that undermines adulthood, yet it's impossible to create another society without a fairly large number of responsible adults. Kant knew his solution could only be partial: growing up will never be complete. It's the work of generations, for each of us is limited by an education we could not choose, from which we can, at best, take something of value, and only free ourselves partly from the rest. In 1968 the philosopher Herbert Marcuse even wrote: 'All education today is therapy: therapy in the sense of liberating man by all available means from a society in which, sooner or later, he is going to be transformed into a brute, even if he doesn't notice it any more.'[31]

But even partial liberation will leave the next generation a better place to start. Acknowledging that your best efforts to think and act autonomously will never entirely reach fruition, without acknowledging this as defeat, is part of growing up. It may even be misleading to think of the process as growing *up*, a metaphor that begins from the physical growth of childhood but encourages us to think of life as a path leading steadily towards the top of a great peak till we disappear into the clouds or slide down the other side, depending on our religious affiliation, or lack thereof. But the path isn't steady. You reach a peak that turns out to be a foothill, steel yourself quickly to go down for a spell to walk the plateau, until you can begin to ascend again to the top of what you're sure is now the real peak at last. One kind of success or another. The older you get, the more you know that the plateaus are not endless, the plunges rarely fatal. If you prefer to think in other modes of travel – for the metaphor of life as a journey is a very old one – you may like to think of yourself in Neurath's boat: 'We are like sailors who have to rebuild their ship on the open sea, without ever being able to dismount it in dry dock and reconstruct it from its best components.'[32]

Every analytic philosopher has heard this quote in an introductory course in epistemology or philosophy of science, and they will have heard that it was written by the Austrian philosopher Otto Neurath, one of the men who founded the Vienna Circle, often considered the birthplace of analytic philosophy. It's unlikely they were told that it was first noticed in a book he wrote in prison, or that it is part of a book called *Anti-Spengler*. Neurath dedicated the book to 'the young and the future they shape' against the best-selling *Decline of the West*, in which Oswald Spengler presented a two-volume argument for downfall and doom.

Neurath chose a different path. In addition to writing and teaching logic, political economy, philosophy of science and sociology, he was a leader in developing housing for low-income workers, as well as the founder of the Viennese Museum for Social and Economic Affairs. His most passionate projects involved education, and he invented a system of graphic design for use in adult education that's still influential today. Those are just the highlights. A lifelong left-wing

Social Democrat, Neurath found himself in prison when the short-lived Bavarian Soviet Republic, whose office for economic planning he directed, was overthrown. After travels that embraced New York as well as Moscow, he left Vienna when Austria was annexed by the Nazis, and lived in exile in Holland and England. The sheer variety and intensity of his activities reveal a man who refused to give in to Spenglerian or any other messages to resign himself to accepting the flailing world he was given. His life may be as good a model for grown-ups as was his famous metaphor.

Certain readers will baulk at this point, if they haven't already baulked before. *It's all very well for some . . . energetic types, but if that's the sort of life you call grown-up, most people do not want it.* They may not think that growing up entails wearing a tie or a serious (as in 'dour') expression, but they sense the demands that real thinking for oneself would make on them, and they'd prefer to spend their time on the couch surfing, thank you very kindly. *What can you say to them?* Rousseau's *Social Contract* contains the unfortunate sentence 'men must be forced to be free', but he knew as well as any that freedom and force are at odds. We do speak of people who are forced to grow up, when war or abandonment or family tragedy prematurely thrusts them into responsibilities they should not have to accept. But nobody recommends it, for it's just as likely to produce people who are bitter and fearful as the self-determined courageous adults whom we need.

Maturity cannot be commanded, it must be desired. What we can offer is not force but persuasion, presenting models that are more compelling than the ones we now know. What's needed is not rage against the dying of the light, but *pace* Dylan Thomas, rage against the picture of ageing as one of dying light. For some lights glow even brighter.

The sheer passage of time brings with it experience, and with it perspective. This isn't yet wisdom, but it's usually the case that perspective brings pleasures the young do not know. The last ten years have seen a flood of studies in which psychologists and economists report a finding that's surprising in light of the view that coming of age is a lesson in disappointment: most people become happier as they grow older. These studies range from the Grant study, which conducted in-depth interviews with Harvard men over fifty years, to less meticulous but broader investigations of people across seventy-two countries. Most of them report what's been dubbed the U-Bend: people become increasingly unhappy until middle age – the average global low point occurs at forty-six, though there is wide variation among nations, with the Swiss hitting bottom at thirty-five and the Ukrainians at sixty-two – at which point they report becoming steadily happier. Researchers controlled for all the obvious factors – income, employment, children – and found they didn't matter. Regardless of social or economic standing, people report that their lives are happier as they grow older. The empirical evidence is constant from the United States to Zimbabwe.

The findings have sent scientists scrambling for explanations. One study used brain scans to argue that older people have reduced memory for negative images, suggesting that the ageing hippocampus selects rosier experiences and suppresses the rest. Another study compared the reactions of thirty-year-olds and seventy-year-olds to recordings of people who were disparaging them. While both groups reported sadness, only the young were really angry about it, suggesting that older people learn to manage emotion more smoothly. Both these explanations may contain some truth. Cynics can read the results as a result of diminished expectations: we become happier because we become happier with less. Most psychologists admit that we simply do not know why, in a world that portrays growing up as a process of decline – of hopes and joys as well as the physical capacity to realize them – so many empirical studies report the opposite.

They also report a good deal of growth. The American philosopher and psychologist William James was simply wrong when he wrote in 1890 that, 'In most of us, by the age of 30, the character has set like plaster, and will never soften again.'[33] Gail Sheehy and George Vaillant, for example, began their different long-term studies of the life cycle with the assumption that people stopped growing up in their fifties. Their subjects taught them better. Vaillant reports a seventy-five-year-old who was almost indignant: he knew he'd only grown better – and happier, in part because he knew it – the older he'd grown. His bones may have come to 'ache in the places where I used to play', as Leonard Cohen so precisely put it. But he was still engaged in becoming the person he wanted to be, and his life was full of meaning that he hadn't found before.[34]

Even in a culture that works against growing up, we grow older without trying, and in that process we can't help but grow up part way. As we do, we discover the things that get better. Aesthetic pleasure becomes more intense. In childhood you hear that you're meant to enjoy sunsets, but you're too busy exploring to sit still and gaze. Later you reject emotions you are meant to feel, and learn to call them kitsch. As you grow up you no longer care if that sunset in that moment would seem kitschy if seen through other eyes. You see it with yours, and you're simply grateful to witness. The same is true with great art or good music. The Roman philosopher Cicero found it in his garden:

I say nothing here of the natural force which all things propagated from the earth possess – the earth which from that tiny grain in a fig, or the grape-stone in a grape, or the most minute seeds of the other cereals and plants, produces such huge trunks and boughs. Mallet-shoots, slips, cuttings, quicksets, layers – are they not enough to fill anyone with delight and astonishment? (*Old Age*, pp. 64–5)

He continues at some length to describe the ordinary miracle we call a grapevine before concluding 'Can anything be richer in product or more beautiful to contemplate?' (Ibid) The intense simplicity of aesthetic pleasure increases as other forms of sensual pleasure change. You still feel lust, and fulfil it, but it no longer has the force of domination it had in your youth. Plato's *Republic* begins with a story about the poet Sophocles who was asked: 'How about your service of Aphrodite, Sophocles – is your natural force still unabated?' And he replied, 'Hush, man, most gladly have I escaped this thing you talk of, as if I had run away from a raging and savage beast of a master.' You may incline to pity Sophocles, and remind yourself that he was, after all, a *tragic* poet. But did you never make a romantic decision – often the most important decisions we ever make – out of lust you were certain was love? Growing up means realizing that no time of one's life is the best one, and resolving to savour every second of joy within reach. You know each will pass, and you no longer experience that as betrayal.

Do we grow more courageous as we grow up? Cicero says that old age is more confident and courageous than youth because the old have come to disregard death. Sometimes, perhaps, but it's often rather because we recognize that everyone else is as terrified of being found wanting, and faking it, as we are. Those who looked braver than you felt were feeling what you did, they just whistled louder in the dark. The confidence that arises when you grasp that is itself a source of pleasure. You may begin to understand what Kant meant by saying you have duties to yourself, and the basis of these is dignity, preserving the idea of humanity in your own person (*Lectures on Pedagogy*, pp. 475–6). Life will still surprise you – if it doesn't you are lost – but you learn to trust your own responses to it. You've begun to construct a story about how the pieces of your life fit together. The story will be revised more than once, and become increasingly coherent, if not always increasingly true, giving shape to your life as it goes on. Places and objects will make it resonate. (The street corner on which you couldn't help crying heartbroken over a love affair you can now recount as an interesting anecdote. The basket you bought from a market woman who taught you something about her continent. The painted bird made by a friend who ended the friendship twenty years ago for reasons neither of you would remember if you met on the street today.)

The ability to see your life as the whole it has become allows you to see the strengths with which you've lived it, and develop a sense of your own character. For integrity is never static; it's too easy to lose for that. It's rather a matter of determination: you've begun to figure out what sort of person you want to be, and you resolve to work harder to become it. In doing this you care far less about what people think of you, though you may be more useful to them. Every psychologist who talks about life cycles talks about what Erikson called generativity: the satisfaction that comes from giving back to the world the better things it gave to you, and especially of nurturing the young. You may discover the pleasure of generosity. You can give a gift or an honest compliment without fearing it will be viewed as flattery, you no longer view constant criticism as a sign of intelligence.

For your intelligence has likely improved. Kant divided the workings of our mind into several different functions. This wasn't a new sort of project, nor is it an old-fashioned one, as the flurry of neurosciences makes clear, but little yet discovered by neuroscience makes Kant's study of mind obsolete. Showing which part of your brain lights up when you think this or that does not show you how conscious thinking functions. Plato tried out models that reflect how we think, and modern philosophers since Descartes spent considerable energy trying to understand how the mind works. They described differences between reasoning, imagining, intuiting, understanding, judging, common sense and a host of other intellectual activities in taxonomies that were as diverse as they were fluid. A number of those taxonomies were explicitly written as textbooks guided by a simple assumption: understanding how we think will make us think better, and who could be opposed to that? Kant's goals were similar, if more ambitious, though his explanation of how the mind works was more careful and systematic than that of his predecessors – if never quite as systematic as he or his critics believed.

His most important work, the *Critique of Pure Reason*, divides the mind into three basic functions. Through sensibility we receive raw data in space and time; through understanding we process that data into objects with mass and substance and other qualities; only by using reason do we actually think about them. As we saw in chapter 2, it is reason's removal from simple knowledge of reality that allows it to step back and ask why reality is this way rather than that – the condition on creative activity and social change alike. Whether or not you actually get them, it is reasonable to expect justice and joy. What makes you condemn parts of reality is not a childish inclination to daydream, but the first law of reason itself. The principle of sufficient reason is simply the demand that the world should make sense. Injustice does not.

All this is clear enough in the *Critique of Pure Reason*, if you actually read the whole book. Long before those like Bertrand Russell begin to nod off, however, Kant introduces another faculty of mind. In contrast to his careful, and sometimes longwinded discussion of sensibility, understanding and reason, his discussion of judgement is remarkably short. He tells us that it's the capacity to apply principles to particular cases, and calls it a peculiar talent that can be practised but not taught, 'and its lack no school can make good' (A133/B172). To teach a principle for applying principles would begin an infinite regress, for how do you know when and where to apply that one? Our experience is particular. I don't experience a tree in general, but the linden losing its browning leaves before my window. Nor will principles of morality do much good if I cannot determine whether *this* act is honourable or *that* one despicable. Without judgement, you may understand a universal principle without ever being able to determine whether a particular case falls under it or not. About such people Kant adds the only (faintly) funny footnote in the entire first *Critique*:

> Deficiency in judgment is just what is ordinarily called stupidity, and for such a failing there is no remedy. An obtuse or narrow-minded person to whom nothing is wanting save a proper degree of understanding and the concepts appropriate thereto, may indeed be trained through study, even to the extent of becoming learned. But as such people are commonly still lacking in judgment, it is not unusual to meet learned men who in the application of their scientific knowledge betray that original want, which can never be made good. (A135/B173)

There's a reason Kant's work is studded with legal metaphors. A good judge has studied the law and knows all its general principles. Her job is to listen to a series of reasonable arguments, then withdraw, reflect and make a decision: it wasn't murder, it was manslaughter. Without judgement reason is paralysed, unable to apply its ideas to the world. Kant is often ridiculed as rule-bound, particularly with regard to his moral philosophy. His categorical imperative – the moral law that tells us to treat other people not as means to our ends but as ends in themselves – is often caricatured as a sort of machine that grinds out rules that tell us just how to act. But while treating people as ends and not means is a fine general principle, deciding whether you are doing so in a particular situation is enormously complex. That Kant understood this as well as anyone is clear in this example from his *Metaphysics of Morals*:

> An author asks one of his readers, 'How do you like my work?' One could merely seem to give an answer by joking about the impropriety of the question. But who has his wit always ready? The author will take the slightest hesitation in answering as an insult. May one, then, say what is expected of one?

His more often read (yes, it's shorter) *Foundation of the Metaphysics of Morals* leads readers to conclude he thought lying was always immoral. Here he shows how any ordinary social dilemma can be an occasion to think for yourself. Kant never tells us what we should say to the author, though the example does suggest that authors ought to spare their readers such situations, even with such an innocuous question as 'Have you had a chance to read it yet?' The example is meant for the reader to figure out.

It is judgement, in short, that plays the most important role in thinking, for it is judgement that decides which thought (which idea, which concept, which principle) applies to which piece of the world. Judgement makes the leap between theory and practice. Kant decided his first great taxonomy gave it too short a shrift, for almost twenty years after the *Critique of Pure Reason* he published the *Critique of Judgement* (1790). In it he tells us that good judgement is so important and necessary that it usually goes by the name of common sense. The book has provided occupation for scholars ever since, for though full of important ideas about teleology, taste and aesthetics, it's hard to see how it's meant to answer the question the first *Critique* left open. It distinguishes between determinant judgements, which subsume particular things under general rules, and reflective judgements, which derive general rules from particulars, but Kant tells us little about how to make them. Is there anything more to be said about judgement other than it can't be taught but only practised, and that people who lack it are those we call stupid?

Among her other achievements, Arendt was one of the great neo-Kantians; few people understood his work better, especially his conviction that our concepts of reason and judgement have political consequences. She too was raised in Königsberg, though she left the city early and travelled far. Perhaps it helped give her the nerve to do what nobody else ever ventured: to write last works planned to mirror all three of Kant's great *Critiques*. She finished *Thinking* and *Willing*, which paralleled Kant's critiques of pure and practical reason. When she died of a heart attack in 1975, the first page of *Judging* was in her typewriter. Those who hoped Arendt might explicate what Kant did not can only groan, but it's hard to imagine that she would have been able to fill out much more than Kant did – because of the peculiar nature of judgement itself. Her *Lectures on Kant's Political Philosophy* do provide some useful thoughts about it while expounding her basic concepts of natality and plurality: the fact that we are born and the fact that there is more than one of us. She stresses the political nature of Kant's theory of mind, for he holds sociability to be the origin of our humanity:

> This is a radical departure from all those theories that stress human interdependence as dependence on our fellow men for our *needs* and *wants*. Kant stresses that at least one of our *mental faculties*, the faculty of judgment, presupposes the presence of others. (*Lectures on Kant*, p. 74)

In radical opposition to every philosopher who came before him, Kant believed that philosophy was not an exercise for the privileged few, but an activity prescribed by the very nature of reason itself – hence something that's natural to all of us. For all philosophy is an attempt to wrestle with three questions that concern us all: what can I know? What should I do? What may I hope? Later Kant wrote that all these questions could be reduced to another: what is the human being? The *Critique of Pure Reason* makes the astonishingly radical claim that its conclusions are confirmed by the fact that they are just as available to the common understanding as to the philosophers:

> For we have thereby revealed to us, what could not at the start have been foreseen, namely, that in matters which concern all men without distinction nature is not guilty of any partial distribution of her gifts, and that in regard to the essential ends of human nature the highest philosophy cannot advance further than is possible under the guidance which nature has bestowed even upon the most ordinary understanding. (A831/B859)

Some common understanding, you may be inclined to snort, all the more upon learning that the passage just quoted occurs on page 831 of the *Critique*'s first edition. It's preceded by many that are far more impenetrable. Kant's own judgement of the book's style was unswerving. He called it 'dry, obscure, opposed to all usual concepts and moreover long-winded' (*Prolegomena*, p. 3). I began by quoting Kant's wistful comment that it isn't given to everyone to write as well as the writers he admired. It's doubtless easier to write well if you grow up in a home filled with good books and articulate people. Still Rousseau's father was also a craftsman, and he taught himself to write gorgeous prose. There is no way around it: apart from an occasional stunning sentence, Kant's work is hard to read. But like learning an instrument or another language, the effort to do so is worth it, for the lesson that remains after cutting through the tangle of words is meant for all of us. *You can enlarge your mind.*

What does all of this have to do with persuading people to grow up? Judgement is the ability that normally requires age to improve. Writers from Cicero to contemporary psychologists are in agreement: your memory will acquire blank spots, your performance on cognitive tests depending solely on speed will decline. But in everything related to judgement, your thinking is likely to improve. Kant's understanding of judgement explains it. For how can it be learned if it cannot be taught? 'By comparing our judgement with the possible rather than the actual judgements of others, and by putting ourselves in the place of any other man' (*Critique of Judgement*, §40). You enlarge your mind by continually thinking from others' perspectives, stepping into as many pairs of shoes as you can find. Let Neurath's boat be your guide. As your judgement improves, so will your ability to learn, travel and work in ways that minimize the pitfalls we saw. And the more you learn where you can, travel freely, find work that you cherish, the better your judgement will be. Call it a virtuous circle: there is no straight path that will take you there.

Ideally, you develop good judgement by watching other people who have it, but you can learn from bad examples as well. Since judgement is about particulars, examples are crucial, though deciding which ones are truly exemplary of something important, and which ones are simply oddballs, is a matter of judgement itself. All this takes time (and preferably space: the right kind of travel does give you access to more people's judgement, thus improving your own). As de Beauvoir explains in *The Coming of Age*:

> In many fields, such as philosophy, ideology and politics, the elderly man is capable of a synthetic vision forbidden to the young. In order to be able to appreciate the importance or unimportance of some particular exception to the rule or allot it its place, to subordinate details to the whole, and to set anecdote aside in order to isolate the general idea, one must have observed an enormous number of facts in all

their aspects of likeness and difference. And there is one form of experience that belongs only to the old – that of old age itself. The young have only vague and erroneous notions of it. (p. 381)

Growing older, of course, is not a sufficient condition for having good judgement: we've all met old fools. Nor is it absolutely necessary: occasionally, Australian Aborigine peoples will appoint young men to be elders – not because they know so many of the old stories that serve to orient the community, but because they know which stories to tell when. In general, however, growing up leads to better judgement, as good judgement is generally a sign of being grown-up. For more than you may fear – if less than you may hope – is in your hands. Even Cicero, who knows his praise of old age is unusual, reminds us that: 'Throughout my discourse remember that my panegyric applies to old age that has been established on foundations laid by youth' (*Old Age*, p. 68). This is not a reference to stopping smoking or starting to exercise, though Cicero, presumably, would advise you to do both. More important: you can lose judgement, like any other capacity, if you fail to use it.

But how to use it well when none of the distinguished old philosophers will offer any guidelines? There's no question about it: *think for yourself*, Kant's motto for maturity, is undeniably vague. But how could it be made more specific without violating the message itself? By telling someone how to do it in any situation she might encounter? Exactly. To tell someone how to think for herself is to undermine the possibility of her doing it at all. The *Critique of Judgement* does make suggestions that are slightly more determinate. 'Think for oneself (the maxim of enlightenment); Put oneself in thought in the place of everyone else (the maxim of the enlarged mentality); and the maxim of consistency, Be in agreement with oneself' (§40). This may not seem like much to go on, but Kant's maxim of consistency does point towards some guidance. What would it mean to be in agreement with yourself?

Would you live your life over if given the chance? Like most interesting questions, this one has haunted the West for almost 2,500 years, but Enlightenment thinkers took it up with special relish. No wonder: they were living in the first time in memory when individual human lives became the subject of change. Had you lived before the Enlightenment, your life would have been largely determined by your father's father's father's, and his place as a slave or free man in a social structure that seemed as set in stone as the great cathedrals it produced. Once life was no longer viewed as given by God and fixed in place by social and political forces that claimed to have His blessing, the question of whether you'd choose yours began to make sense.

Few Enlightenment thinkers were entirely clear about the kind of question they were asking. Was it an empirical enquiry about how many people would in fact choose to live their lives over, with the same end as the sorts of happiness studies that social scientists undertake today? Or was it rather a philosophical question of whether life, on balance, is justified? All the answers they left us hover between the two. On the cusp of the Enlightenment, the notoriously optimistic Leibniz held a surprising position. He thought most people at the point of death (if they had no knowledge of heaven) would take up their lives again, but only on the condition that their lives, if no better, would be different next time round. We would insist on variety before agreeing to go through this again. Voltaire was as usual more caustic. He agreed that most of us on our deathbeds would choose to take our lives back, but this is just about fear of dying. Even then, we'd insist on variety too: better to die of anything else than to die of boredom. Voltaire wrote poems in praise of pleasure and luxury throughout his long life, and clearly enjoyed a great deal of both. He also had more than an ordinary share of life's deeper joys: more than one real love story, plenty of friends and admirers and the knowledge that his voluminous work had an impact on the wider world. Yet in the same book – *Zadig* – that insists the world is a much better place than its detractors complain, he gleefully recounts a myth that describes the earth as a toilet where the slops of the universe are dumped. The fact that we cling on our deathbeds to lives we've done little but complain of is, he believes, just one more proof that humankind is mad.

Hume agreed that this is folly, but his view was even more cheerless than Voltaire's. (Hume's unique ability to promote a bleak view of humankind with a sort of jovial elegance allows his admirers to overlook the fact that only Schopenhauer's view is bleaker.) Ever playing the part of empiricist, Hume claimed to be merely reporting:

> Ask yourself, ask any of your acquaintances, whether they would live over again the last ten or twenty years of their life. No! But the next twenty, they say, will be better . . . Thus at last they find (such is the greatness of human misery; it reconciles even contradictions!) that they complain, at once, of the shortness of life, and of its vanity and sorrow. (*Dialogues Concerning Natural Religion*, pp. 99–100)

Rousseau thought such statements were their problem, not his. He was convinced that well-fed, well-bred men like Voltaire and Hume create their own misery. How can anyone blessed with Voltaire's many fortunes find the world wretched, while Rousseau 'in obscurity, poor, alone, tormented by a suffering without remedy, I meditate with pleasure on my retreat and find that all is well' (Letter to Voltaire, 18 August 1756). Yet though he insists that, unlike the overstuffed Parisians, every mountaineer in Valais would choose to repeat his life endlessly, Rousseau's own choice is not entirely clear. Few people wrote more poignant descriptions of happiness, or more enthusiastically, on occasion, of their own. But he often repeated that life always holds more suffering than happiness – even in the book he considered his brightest, *Emile*.

Kant's discussion of the question also veers between reporting what we would choose, and considering what we should. In 'The End of All Things' he mentions Voltaire's Persian legend of the earth as a toilet, and adds a couple of others: earth as prison, as madhouse, as cheap highway inn. He claims to be merely repeating metaphors others have used. But other texts suggest he found a desire to repeat one's life over to be positively irrational:

> The value of life for us, if it is estimated by *that which we enjoy* (that is, by happiness), is easy to decide. It sinks below zero; for who would be willing to enter upon life anew under the same conditions? Who would do so even under a new, self-chosen plan (yet in conformity with the course of nature) if it were merely directed to enjoyment? (*Critique of Judgement*, §83)

He goes on to dismiss the argument that, after all, most people prefer living to dying:

> one can leave an answer to this sophistry to the good sense of each man who has lived long enough and

reflected on the value of life; you have only to ask him whether he would be willing to play the game of life once more, not under the same conditions, but under any conditions of our earthly world and not those of some fairy-land.[35]

That's life seen as an object of pleasure; thank heaven we have duty! Without it, Kant is certain that not only would few of us live our lives over; most of us would be tempted to suicide.

The Enlightenment, in short, was never as sanguine or sunny as its critics suppose. These men wrote reams of pages about evil, and their conclusions about a world that contains so much of it were often sombre. It's hard to know whether their reflections on reliving one's life were meant to be surveys, soliloquies or parlour games. A century later, however, Nietzsche turned the question into a cornerstone of his philosophy. His *Twilight of the Idols* states: 'In every age the wisest have passed the identical judgment on life: *it is Worthless* . . . Everywhere and always their mouths have uttered the same sound – a sound full of doubt, full of melancholy, full of weariness with life, full of opposition to life' (p. 29). Nietzsche believed this was a form of revenge. The sages themselves were weak and decadent. Unequal to the challenges that living presents, they sought to spoil it for the rest of us by inventing another life that makes this one look like a tale of woe. 'Why a Beyond if not as a means of befouling the Here-and-Now?' (Ibid). Christianity is the clearest case of this inversion, but Nietzsche called Christianity the Platonism of the masses; he thought every philosophy before his leads us to despise life itself.

So he proposed a test. Don't think of time, or your own life within it, as something linear, leading upwards or forwards to a point of redemption. Imagine instead something circular: moments that recur eternally, ever again. Face the particulars: think of pain and heart-break and all the things that make you wonder on occasion if you'd be better off dead. Could you live that life, with all its contents and contingencies, over and over for all eternity? If you say yes you are stronger than the Stoics, who merely urged us to accept our fate. Nietzsche challenges us to love it. Your answer to the question is the key to your soul. Forceful, noble spirits can affirm the eternal return of the life they are living; slavish, resentful ones will shrink from the idea in horror.

Nietzsche sometimes presents the eternal return as a piece of cosmology. I have argued elsewhere that it is instead a very powerful counter-theology, though it is infected by both the Stoicism and the Christianity Nietzsche claims to despise.[36] But Nietzsche's test can serve us as a tool. Supposing you asked yourself regularly: would I live *this* life over? (Not over and over, as Nietzsche demanded. Once would be enough.) If the answer looks like Hume's did – not the last ten years, but the next will surely be better – then you'd better get to work. How many of the choices you've made are truly fixed? What parts of your life are changeable, and what do you want to keep? This is not a matter of glorified New Year's resolutions, but of asking of yourself the same questions you must ask of your parents and your culture if you're in earnest about growing up. *Which parts are really mine?* If you are carrying around inheritances of which you never truly took possession, you do not even know how little you are thinking for yourself.

I get the idea. Being in agreement with oneself, Kant's maxim of consistency, can be furthered if we consistently ask if this life is the one we want to be living, and doing something about it if the answer is no. But isn't the problem less with the life we've lived so far than the one that is certainly before us? Don't people refuse to grow up because growing up means growing old?

It does, if you're lucky. The alternative is dying young.

The men who sang 'Hope I die before I get old' were not in fact talking about their generation; it's a very old sentiment. De Beauvoir's *The Coming of Age* dates its written expression back to the philosopher and poet Ptah-hotep who lived in Egypt in 2500 B.C.E.

How hard and painful are the last days of an aged man! He grows weaker every day; his eyes become dim, his ears deaf; his strength fades; his heart knows peace no longer; his mouth falls silent and he speaks no word. The power of his mind lessens and today he cannot remember what yesterday was like. All his bones hurt. Those things which not long ago were done with pleasure are painful now; and taste vanishes. Old age is the worst of misfortunes that can afflict a man. (*The Coming of Age*, p. 92)

De Beauvoir's ambitious study explores ageing from inside and out, examining both social practices and attitudes towards the aged as well as differing individuals' own perceptions of ageing from prehistoric times through to the mid-twentieth century. It can make for disconcerting reading, for in almost every generation there's a written consensus: growing old is worse than death. There are some exceptions. *The Coming of Age* spans cultures in which the old are ceremonially killed or abandoned and those in which being called old is a sign of respect and honour. On the whole, de Beauvoir shows that the better the place of children in a culture, the better the place of the elderly, for the bonds formed between well-treated children and their parents are strong enough to resist the temptation to discard the less productive elderly – even in nomadic societies where ageing bodies are not only a drain on scarce resources but an impediment to the movement of the group as a whole. Still, she argues, the problem of ageing is that the status of the old is never won, but granted by the young, as her book *The Second Sex* argued that women's standing is granted by men. De Beauvoir emphasizes the great variety in ageing among people of different classes. While well-educated, well-off creative people may indeed lead creative, expanding lives well into their eighties, the old worker's world shrinks. This is not merely a matter of poverty, though she steers our attention to those in whom activity is thwarted for lack of money to buy a bus ticket or a beer at the local pub. Even worse:

> The tragedy of old age is tantamount to a fundamental condemnation of a whole mutilating system of life that provides the immense majority of those who make part of it with no reason for living. Labor and weariness hide this void; it becomes apparent as soon as they have retired. It is far more serious than boredom. Once the worker has grown old he no longer has any place on earth because in fact he was never given one. No place; but he had no time to realize it. When he does discover the truth he falls into a kind of bewildered despair. (*The Coming of Age*, p. 274)

De Beauvoir's account of the tragedy of old age is remarkably similar to Goodman's account of the tragedy of adolescence. We have not created a world in which reasonable people should want to grow up, or grow old. Unsurprisingly, her conclusion is similar to his:

Old age exposes the failure of our entire civilization. It is the whole man that must be remade, it is the whole relationship between man and man that must be recast if we wish the old person's state to be acceptable . . . It is the whole system that is at issue and our claim cannot be otherwise than radical – change life itself. (Ibid, p. 543)

De Beauvoir is right to insist that the problems of ageing are at least as social in origin as they are biological. Her own comparison of the status of the aged to the status of women leaves real space for hope. It's easy to point to sexist structures that remain in the twenty-first century, and in parts of the world they can still be fatal. Yet it's undeniable that the relationships between men and women have changed more in the last fifty years than in all the centuries before them, put together. We are now exploring possibilities between genders that de Beauvoir could hardly imagine, even as *The Second Sex* was one of the books that contributed to expanding possibility's scope. As life expectancies and economic structures change we may find ourselves echoing Rousseau's 'We do not *know* what our nature permits us to be' and follow him in testing its limits.

But even for those who do their best to think for themselves, possibilities will be affected by others' expectations. De Beauvoir's account of the urge to ridicule old age, bolstered with quotations that span every historical period since ancient Greece and Rome, is as chilling as it's puzzling. It's easier to understand some men's continuing contempt for women and some societies' continuing disrespect for their minorities than it is to understand the mixture of disdain, derision and revulsion which marks so many discussions of the aged. For unlike being a woman or having different coloured skin, old age is a fate that awaits us all. If we're lucky.

Fine examples can be found in the outpouring of mocking that, today, greets the information that a major rock star has reached a round-numbered birthday or opened a concert tour. Here is a quote from a recent *New York Times*:

> Just look at them: the graybeards and grannies smoking pot, the bodies tugged by gravity and wretched excess, all that late-age libido and feeble jump-stepping enabled by Viagra and Lipitor. Baby boomers – a stadium full of them. Is there anything worse? . . . Where is the off-ramp marked grace, dignity or class for the 76 million Americans born between 1946 and 1964?[37]

European media can, if possible, be even nastier in asking: isn't it time for these people to accept their obsolescence and leave the stage to others? I have often wondered why the fact that some of the greatest talents of our time refuse to get off stage should fill people with rage – particularly since, as anyone who has actually seen recent concerts of Bob Dylan, Leonard Cohen or Bruce Springsteen will know, they are anything but laughable. On the contrary, each of these artists has shown how far human and creative development can continue, surviving flops and falls and excess and error – and thus provides a model of how to grow up. Can it be that these men produce resentment because we are too lazy, or frightened, to grow up ourselves? Or are we complicit in sending a message to the young (and internalizing it ourselves) about what life can hold? Those between eighteen and thirty are continuously told that they are living the best years of their lives, though it's the decade that is often the hardest – and it has only got harder as structuring norms and economic stability dissolve. But rather than being encouraged to react to the complex doubt and struggle of those years by determining to grow out of them, the young only hear that no grown-up state will be better. 'Enjoy the best years of your lives' sounds cheery, but it contains an ominous message: everything else will be worse.

Take a look at most any discussion of coming of age and you'll find a reference to something called 'Shakespeare's seven ages of man'; google it, as of this writing, and you will get 196 million entries. In fact, dividing the life cycle into seven ages began well before Shakespeare, but most people will recognize the very famous line with which the speech begins:

'All the world's a stage'. The line that follows is grim enough: all the men and women are *merely* players, suggesting that the script of our lives has been written and the parts are all fixed. Worse than that: every possible role we might play is both miserable and ridiculous. The baby's part is to mewl and puke, the schoolboy whines on his way to school, the lover can but sigh, writing foolheaded verse, the soldier seeks the glory that will kill him, and so it goes through to the last pathetic sequence that leaves the player with nothing at all. Here is the speech in full:

> All the world's a stage,
> And all the men and women merely players:
> They have their exits and their entrances;
> And one man in his time plays many parts,
> His acts being seven ages. At first the infant,
> Mewling and puking in the nurse's arms.
> And then the whining school-boy, with his satchel,
> And shining morning face, creeping like snail
> Unwillingly to school. And then the lover,
> Sighing like furnace, with a woeful ballad
> Made to his mistress' eyebrow. Then a soldier,
> Full of strange oaths, and bearded like the pard,
> Jealous in honour, sudden and quick in quarrel,
> Seeking the bubble reputation
> Even in the cannon's mouth. And then the justice,
> In fair round belly with good capon lin'd,
> With eyes severe, and beard of formal cut,

Full of wise saws and modern instances;
And so he plays his part. The sixth age shifts
Into the lean and slipper'd pantaloon,
With spectacles on nose, and pouch on side;
His youthful hose, well sav'd, a world too wide
For his shrunk shank; and his big manly voice,
Turning again toward childish treble, pipes
And whistles in his sound. Last scene of all,
That ends this strange eventful history,
Is second childishness and mere oblivion, –
Sans teeth, sans eyes, sans taste, sans everything.

(*As You Like It*, Act II, scene 7)

A more formidable gloss on the modern slogan *life sucks and then you die* would be hard to find.

Now some of the texts that quote it try to soften Shakespeare's blows. *Psychology Today* points out that people live longer than they did in his day; we can go to the gym and take advantage of modern dentistry. Others latch on to the gloom with something like glee. Shakespeare being rightly considered a source of general wisdom – including the insight that there are more things in heaven and earth than philosophy can ever dream of – the view that human life is both futile and absurd gains authority through his bitter and brilliant expression. To be sure, as Kant taught us, reason has the right, and even the obligation to question authority; this view of coming of age might indeed be Shakespeare's and nevertheless be wrong. Still I blanched on reading the speech, for crossing swords with Shakespeare is daunting. I reached for my copy of *As You Like It*, for it had been decades since I'd seen it, and I no longer remembered the context.

It was a revelation. For the speech is spoken by the courtier Jacques, who says of himself 'I can suck melancholy out of a song, as a weasel sucks eggs'. His description of his own melancholy is so melancholic that it turns out to be funny, which is why none of the other characters in the play take him seriously. His melancholy, finally, is a comic device. The fact that Jacques' melancholy is so extreme as to be ludicrous does not make him dispensable. Without him, the play's second half would be sappy. His voice counts, for this is the real world, not just Arcadia, or the forest of Ardennes. Shakespeare's wisdom consists in the fact that he can express such voices perfectly – as we've seen, such views of life are all too common – and still end the play with a double wedding. It's a comedy, after all.

That Shakespeare is not identifying with but mocking Jacques is underscored by the fact that the famous seven ages speech is spoken just before the entrance of the play's hero, Orlando, bearing the weary servant Adam. Adam's view of ageing is a far cry from Jacques':

> Though I look old, yet I am strong and lusty;
> For in my youth I never did apply
> Hot and rebellious liquors in my blood
>
> (Ibid, Act II, scene 3)

Having followed the sort of advice about moderation in drink and food that could be found in any contemporary manual on successful ageing, Adam concludes: 'Therefore my age is as a lusty winter, / Frosty, but kindly'.

His actions proceed to put the lie to Jacques' picture of the aged as silly and useless, and our lives as pathetic and predetermined journeys. That's to say: Jacques' view of the life cycle gives us no more insight into Shakespeare's own than Lady Macbeth's soliloquies give us insight into Shakespeare's view of morality. Why have generations of readers rushed to identify Jacques' standpoint with Shakespeare's, burnishing the bleakest picture of human existence with the authority of the Bard?

While writing this book I read widely, disparately and so unsystematically that the books I read may have nothing in common but the fact that I learned something or other from each of them. For a year my desk was piled with works on the history of childhood under studies of successful ageing, psychological investigations of the life cycle next to political criticism and sociological treatises sprawled beside *The Picture of Dorian Gray*. Interspersed among them were a number of philosophical works that I knew well enough, but wanted to read again. The disparity suits my conviction that too much contemporary philosophy is marred by isolation from other fields in ways earlier philosophy would have found foreign. (Kant not only read in, but gave university lectures on fields as diverse as geography, anthropology, psychology, mathematics and military strategy – with particular attention to pyrotechnics.) But though no guiding thread tied all subjects together, one difference emerged between those books that were written by philosophers and those that were not. Most of the empirical works aimed to shed a helpful, hopeful light on some piece of the problem of coming of age. They discussed better forms of education or healthier attitudes towards ageing or new modes of political action. They demonstrated how the right sort of vision of the meaning of life could promote soldiers' resistance to combat trauma, or lead to wealth and influence. You're meant to close their pages with the feeling that the problems, if not solved, are certainly manageable. By contrast, the works of philosophy only seemed to make the problems harder. How could that make sense?

I began this book with the claim that philosophy may help us find ways of growing up that do not leave us resigned. It can only do so by way of showing that growing up will be more demanding than we ever imagined. Any philosophical solution of a real problem begins by revealing how far we have ignored it. The American philosopher Stanley Cavell has called philosophy education for grown-ups. His explication makes it clear how it can help us to get there – as well as why it's help we're inclined to reject. For what we need to learn is not a matter of information. 'One could call this learning rethinking, except that this may suggest clarifying (say, giving explanations) which may pass by the essential idea that you *already* know what you keep from yourself' (*Stanley Cavell and the Education of Grownups*, p. 209).

Philosophy seeks answers to questions children raise, and most adults assume have already been answered. *Why should I grow up? Follow rules? Get an education? How do I know? Find meaning? Shape my own life?* These are all questions that can be answered, or dismissed, in a sentence. Yet when you ask them with the attention they actually demand you may find yourself feeling, as Cavell writes, that

> my foregone conclusions were never conclusions *I* arrived at, but were merely imbibed by me, merely conventional. I may blunt that realization through hypocrisy or cynicism or bullying. But I may take the occasion to throw myself back on my culture, and ask why we do what we do, judge as we judge, how we have arrived at these crossroads. What is the natural ground of our convention, to what are they in service? . . . In the face of the questions posed in Augustine, Luther, Rousseau, Thoreau, we are children; we do not know how to go on with them, what ground we may occupy. In this light, philosophy becomes the education of grownups . . . The anxiety

in teaching, in serious communication, is that I myself require education. And for grownups this is not natural growth, but *change*. (*The Claim of Reason*, p. 125)

Philosophy begins by making things harder, and proceeds by showing them as wholes. Each of the questions raised above must be answered individually, but any answer that remains individual will fail. The political dimension is inescapable. It requires us to look beyond even the best-intentioned of interests. As Kant pointed out, it's not just rulers but parents who want to educate children to cope with the world they live in; ideally, however, education would prepare them to help shape a better one. Philosophy, I've said, is inherently normative. Good philosophy recognizes this, while keeping a lookout for all it can learn from descriptions that will inevitably disappoint. Since any description will take place in history, its questions are not eternal, but they have very long lives. So Kant's works can provoke you in ways most works of eighteenth-century science cannot. This is one thing philosophy and literature share in common.

I have argued that the picture of growing up as inevitable decline is supported by a web of interests that operate against our coming of age. The tragedy is the way that we constantly collude in it, seeking confirmation for that picture even where it cannot be found. We misread *As You Like It* to endorse a view that spells our own doom. That's the sort of thing that made Kant call our immaturity self-incurred, and urge us to have the courage to grow out of it. Courage is needed to oppose all the forces that will continue to work against maturity, for real grown-ups are not long distracted by bread and circuses. No longer confused by baubles or shy with inexperience, we are better able to see what we see, and say it. We? All of us, including this author. It's a process of permanent revolution. Who wants to encourage that?

Notes

1. See Peter N. Stearns, *Childhood in World History* (Abingdon: Routledge, 2011).

2. See Catriona Kelly, *Children's World: Growing Up in Russia, 1890–1991* (New Haven, Conn.: Yale University Press, 2007).

3. Immanuel Kant, *Remarks on Observations of the Feeling of the Beautiful and the Sublime (1764–1765)*, in *Kants gesammelte Schrifte,* vol. 20, ed. Königlich Preußische Akademie der Wissenschaft (Berlin: De Gruyter, 1942), p. 44.

4. See Lucie Salwiczek, *Immanuel Kant's Sparrow: High Level Communication in Songbirds and Humans* (Cambridge: Cambridge University Linguistic Society, 2008).

5. Immanuel Kant, *Anthropology from a Pragmatic Point of View,* trans. Robert B. Louden (Cambridge: Cambridge University Press, 2006), p. 124.

6. For a more comprehensive defence of the Enlightenment see Susan Neiman, *Moral Clarity* (London: Vintage, 2011).

7. Jean-Jacques Rousseau, 'Observations', in *The Discourses and Other Early Political Writings*, ed. Victor Gourevitch (Cambridge: Cambridge University Press, 1997), p. 35.

8. For a rejection of standard claims that Rousseau's views of human nature were impossibly utopian, see Neiman, *Moral Clarity*, Chapter 9.

9. I have explored this theme at length in *Evil in Modern Thought* (Princeton, NJ: Princeton University Press, 2004), pp. 78ff.

10. Kant, 'Conjectural Beginning of Human History', trans. Allen W. Wood, in Immanuel Kant, *Anthropology, History, and Education*, eds. Günter Zöller and Robert B. Louden (Cambridge: Cambridge University Press, 2008), pp. 163–75 (p. 168).

11. Ibid, p. 115.

12. Kathleen Freeman, trans., *Ancilla to Pre-Socratic Philosophers: A Complete Translation of the Fragments in Diels*, Fragmente Der Vorsokratiker (Cambridge, Mass.: Harvard University Press, 1948), p. 141.

13. Bernard Williams, *Truth and Truthfulness* (Princeton, NJ: Princeton University Press, 2002).

14. David Hume, *An Enquiry concerning Human Understanding, and Other Writings*, ed. Stephen Buckle (Cambridge: Cambridge University Press, 2007), Book 12, Part 1, Section 34, p. 144.

15. David Hume, *A Treatise of Human Nature*, ed. David Fate Norton and Mary J. Norton (Oxford: Oxford University Press, 2000), Book 3, Part 1, Section 1, p. 302.

16. Ibid, Book 1, Part 4, Section 7, p. 175.

17. Isaiah Berlin, 'Hume and German Anti-Rationalism', in *Against the Current*, ed. Henry Hardy, 2nd edition (Princeton, NJ: Princeton University Press, 2013), p. 235.

18. Boethius, *Consolation of Philosophy*, trans. P. G. Walsh (London: Oxford University Press, 1999), pp. 37–8.

19. Walter Benjamin, 'Dialog über die Religiosität der Gegenwart', in *Benjamin gesammelte Schriften* Vol. II (Frankfurt: Suhrkamp Verlag, 1977), p. 32.

20. J. Darling, *Child-Centred Education and its Critics* (London: Sage Publications, 1993), p. 17.

21. Kant, 'Dessau 1776', *Königsberg Learned and Political Journal*, in Kant, *Anthropology, History, and Education*, eds. Zöller and Louden, p. 100.

22. 'To the Community', in ibid, p. 102.

23. Ibid, p. 104.

24. D. W. Winnicott, 'Transitional objects and transitional phenomena', *The International Journal of Psychoanalysis* 34, 1953.

25. Simone de Beauvoir, *The Ethics of Ambiguity* (New York: Citadel Press, 1948), p. 92.

26. Simone de Beauvoir, *Adieux: A Farewell to Sartre* (New York: Pantheon, 1984), p. 232.

27. George Santayana, 'The Philosophy of Travel', in *The Birth of Reason and Other Essays* (New York: Columbia University Press, 1995), p. 15.

28. Ludwig Wittgenstein, *Philosophical Investigations*, trans. G.E.M. Anscombe (Oxford: Blackwell, 1953), Section 123, p. 49e.

29. Ingo Schulze, *Unsere schönen neuen Kleider* (Berlin: Hanser Berlin, 2012).

30. See, for example, Scott Atran, *Talking to the Enemy: Violent Extremism, Sacred Values, and What it Means to Be Human* (London: Penguin, 2011).

31. Herbert Marcuse, 'Liberation from the Affluent Society', in David Cooper, ed., *The Dialectics of Liberation* (Harmondsworth: Penguin, 1968).

32. Otto Neurath, *Anti-Spengler* (Munich: Georg D. W. Callwey, 1921), p. 199.

33. William James, *The Principles of Psychology*, Vol. 1 (London: Macmillan, 1890), p. 121.

34. George Vaillant, *Triumphs of Experience* (Cambridge, Mass.: Harvard University Press, 2012).

35. Kant, 'On the Impossibility of All Attempts at Theodicy', in Arendt's translation, quoted in her *Lectures on Kant's Political Philosophy*, ed. Ronald Beiner (Chicago: University of Chicago Press, 1982), pp. 24–5.

36. See Neiman, *Evil in Modern Thought*, Chapter 3.

37. Timothy Egan, 'Septuagenarian Strut', NYTimes.com, 25 July 2013, opinionator.blogs.nytimes.com/2013/07/25/septuagenarian-strut/?_php=true&_type=blogs&_r=0.

Index

A Note About the Author

Susan Neiman is the director of the Einstein Forum. Her previous books, translated into many languages, include *Moral Clarity: A Guide for Grown-Up Idealists*, *Evil in Modern Thought: An Alternative History of Philosophy*, *The Unity of Reason: Rereading Kant*, and *Slow Fire: Jewish Notes from Berlin*. She also writes cultural and political commentary for diverse media in the United States, Germany, and Great Britain. Born in Atlanta, Georgia, Neiman studied philosophy at Harvard and the Free University of Berlin and was professor of philosophy at Yale and Tel Aviv Universities. She is the mother of three grown children and lives in Berlin.